Node.js for
.NET Developers

David Gaynes

M000094740

PUBLISHED BY
Microsoft Press
A division of Microsoft Corporation
One Microsoft Way
Redmond, Washington 98052-6399

Library of Congress Control Number: 2015930568
ISBN: 978-0-7356-6298-8

Printed and bound in the United States of America.

First Printing

Microsoft Press books are available through booksellers and distributors worldwide. If you need support related to this book, email Microsoft Press Book Support at mspinput@microsoft.com. Please tell us what you think of this book at http://aka.ms/tellpress.

This book is provided "as-is" and expresses the author's views and opinions. The views, opinions and information expressed in this book, including URL and other Internet website references, may change without notice.

Some examples depicted herein are provided for illustration only and are fictitious. No real association or connection is intended or should be inferred.

Microsoft and the trademarks listed at http://www.microsoft.com on the "Trademarks" webpage are trademarks of the Microsoft group of companies. All other marks are property of their respective owners.

Acquisitions and Developmental Editor: Devon Musgrave
Project Editor: Devon Musgrave
Editorial Production: Waypoint Press (www.waypointpress.com)
Technical Reviewer: Marc Young
Copyeditor: Roger LeBlanc
Indexer: Cristina Yeager
Cover: Twist Creative • Seattle

Contents at a Glance

Table of Contents

What do you think of this book? We want to hear from you!

Microsoft is interested in hearing your feedback so we can continually improve our
books and learning resources for you. To participate in a brief online survey, please visit:

microsoft.com/learning/booksurvey

What do you think of this book? We want to hear from you!

Microsoft is interested in hearing your feedback so we can continually improve our
books and learning resources for you. To participate in a brief online survey, please visit:

microsoft.com/learning/booksurvey

Introduction

Node.js is a JavaScript-based, highly scalable, open-source collection of tools used for sophisticated web development. Using your own chosen set of npm modules woven together under the Node.js paradigm, you can build websites of every imaginable type, from e-commerce to interactive games with multiple simultaneous users. In certain types of web applications, Node.js provides solutions to otherwise challenging technical issues.

Node.js is at its best in real-time web applications that require high-volume, low data-intensive processing of requests or in applications that want to employ push technology using web sockets connections. Today, the vast majority of web applications rely on the stateless request-response paradigm. In this paradigm only the client can initiate communication or data transfer. But with Node.js skills you can quickly build web applications with real-time two-way connections in which both the client and server can initiate communication.

Node.js websites are constructed using the standard open web stack composed of HTML, CSS and JavaScript. It allows for commonly used styling libraries to be added to your chosen collection of npm processing modules. Find out why Node.js is becoming a go-to platform for certain uniquely demanding types of web development.

Who should read this book

This book exists to help current .NET web developers learn the essentials of Node.js web development.

Assumptions

This book expects that you have at least a minimal understanding of .NET development and object-oriented programming concepts. With a heavy focus on web development, this book also assumes that you have a basic understanding of ASP.NET, including the core concepts of web development contained in ASP.NET, such as clients and servers, HTML, CSS, JavaScript, and HTTP post/get. The book also assumes that you have an IDE in which to work, specifically a fairly recent version of Visual Studio.

This book might not be for you if...

This book might not be for you if you have no web programming experience or if your interests within web programming are primarily to desig elegant user interfaces.

Organization of this book

This book is divided into nine chapters, which are designed to walk you through every required aspect of doing node.js development. The first few chapters cover the setup and basics of coding in node.js. The middle section of the book focuses on specific techniques within JavaScript that make life much easier when working with node.js. The last few chapters bring it all together to build a working application from end to end including a few special features, such as token-based authentication.

Conventions and features in this book

This book presents information using conventions designed to make the information readable and easy to follow.

- The book includes command line and JavaScript sample code, clearly separated from standard text

- The book includes references to named open-source modules available on the web. The first reference to each is in bold text

System requirements

You will need the following hardware and software to complete the practice exercises in this book:

- One of Windows XP with Service Pack 3 (except Starter Edition), Windows Vista with Service Pack 2 (except Starter Edition), Windows 7/8/10, Windows Server 2003 with Service Pack 2, Windows Server 2003 R2, Windows Server 2008 with Service Pack 2, or Windows Server 2008 R2.

- Visual Studio 2010 or later, any edition (web developer for Express Edition products).

- SQL Server 2008 Express Edition or higher (2008 or R2 release), with SQL Server Management. Studio 2008 Express or higher (included with Visual Studio, Express Editions require separate download).

- A computer that has a 1.6GHz or faster processor (2GHz recommended).

- 1 GB (32 Bit) or 2 GB (64 Bit) RAM (Add 512 MB if running in a virtual machine or SQL Server Express Editions, more for advanced SQL Server editions).

- 3.5GB of available hard disk space.

- 5400 RPM hard disk drive.

- DirectX 9 capable video card running at 1024 x 768 or higher-resolution display.

- DVD-ROM drive (if installing Visual Studio from DVD).

- Internet connection to download software or chapter examples.

Depending on your Windows configuration, you might require Local Administrator rights to install or configure Visual Studio 2010 and SQL Server 2008 products.

Downloads: Code samples

Most of the chapters in this book include exercises that let you interactively try out new material learned in the main text on your way to building a fully functional web application. Fully working examples of the pages used in the application can be found here:

http://aka.ms/node.js/files

Follow the instructions to download the Nodejs_662988_CompanionContent.zip file.

Using the code samples

The folder created by the setup.exe program contains two kinds of files:

- **JavaScript files**   These files contain the Node. js code that runs your application including navigation, page data content, etc.

■ **EJS files** These files are used in place of standard HTML files for rendering pages. Although they do contain all necessary HTML, they also contain special binding syntax that allows the file to interact with its associated node.js JavaScript file.

Acknowledgments

I'd like to thank the following people: Devon Musgrave and Marc Young for helping me polish this project and get it to print, Devon again for special efforts connected to the project, and of course my wife Samantha for her endless support.

Errata, updates,& book support

We've made every effort to ensure the accuracy of this book and its companion content. You can access updates to this book—in the form of a list of submitted errata and their related corrections—at:

> http://aka.ms/nodejs/errata

If you discover an error that is not already listed, pleasesubmitit to us at the same page.

If you need additional support, email Microsoft Press Book Support at *mspinput@microsoft.com*.

Please note that product support for Microsoft software and hardware is not offered through the previous addresses.For help with Microsoft software or hardware, go to *http://support.microsoft.com*.

Free ebooks from Microsoft Press

From technical overviews to in-depth information on special topics, the free ebooks from Microsoft Press cover a wide range of topics. These ebooks are available in PDF, EPUB, and Mobi for Kindle formats, ready for you to download at:

http://aka.ms/mspressfree

Check back often to see what is new!

We want to hear from you

At Microsoft Press, your satisfaction is our top priority, and your feedback our most valuable asset. Please tell us what you think of this book at:

http://aka.ms/tellpress

We know you're busy, so we've kept it short with just a few questions. Your answers go directly to the editors at Microsoft Press. (No personal information will be requested.) Thanks in advance for your input!

Stay in touch

Let's keep the conversation going! We're on Twitter: *http://twitter.com/MicrosoftPress*

CHAPTER 1

Setup

To begin, head over to NodeJS.org and either just click Install or navigate to the site downloads page where you will see the following:

When you run the .msi file you choose to install, you will see the following:

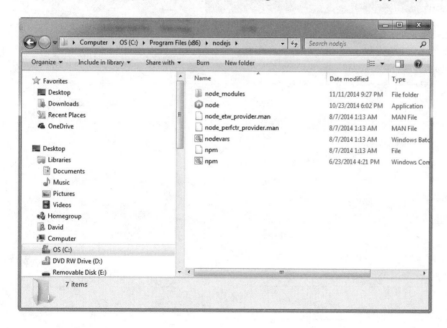

If it all runs properly, you will see the following in whatever directory you specified:

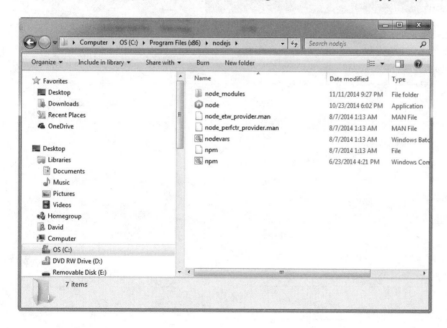

Along with that, you should be able to find a Node.js command prompt in your Start menu. If you click and launch it, you should see this:

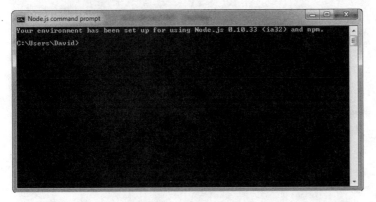

Note how this console entry mentions *npm*. That's the critical package-management application you need to have in place that will enable you to install all the additional packages you will need to more quickly build your Node.js application.

You'll be doing so from the command prompt as shown, just not this specific command prompt. That is because you don't want to have to do it twice. The npm application downloads the necessary packages to the current directory of your command prompt and nowhere else. I will assume that the location just shown is not where your Microsoft Visual Studio projects usually live, and because you are about to wire Node.js to Visual Studio you will want npm to install packages to the directory you will actually be using. Connecting Node.js to your instance of Visual Studio 2010 is not difficult and only involves changing the properties of the project.

> **Tip** If you are using Visual Studio 2012 or later, there is now a plug-in available from Microsoft to create Express versions of Node.js projects. It makes the creation of a Node.js project, or any other JavaScript project, as simple as creating any other kind of project using the standard menu shown here. However, I demonstrate doing so in the absence of the plug-in.

I simply set mine up to start with an empty ASP.NET web application as shown here:

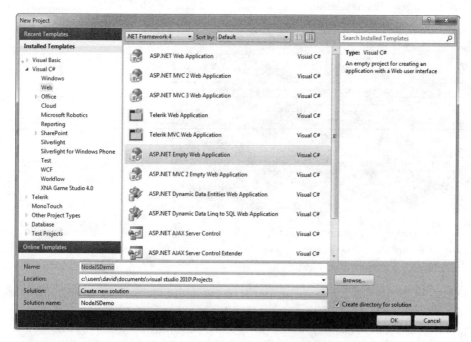

Then I made some quick and easy changes to the properties on the Project tab on your top navigation menu. The specific properties to change can be found on the Web tab, which is the third one from the top:

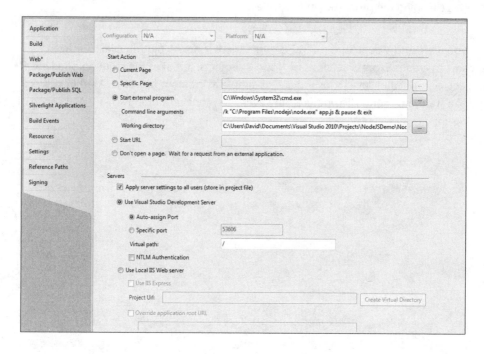

The important section is here:

Start external program	C:\Windows\System32\cmd.exe	...
Command line arguments	/k "C:\Program Files\nodejs\node.exe" app.js & pause & exit	
Working directory	C:\Users\David\Documents\Visual Studio 2010\Projects\NodeJSDemo\Noc	...

It involves four quick steps:

1. Tell Visual Studio to run an external application on startup and not simply a page within your application as usual.

2. Specify the application, including its location and any command-line arguments.

   This is where you refer to the location of your Node.js install.

3. Indicate the arguments and program call exactly as shown.

4. Specify a working directory for all npm package downloads. Typically, this would be the working directory of your web application.

Now you're all set to use Visual Studio for building a Node.js application.

The first step for doing actual development is to start downloading some support npm packages to make your life easier. Again, you can think of an npm package as a third-party DLL—in other words, as a library of ready-made functionality. In .NET, you get a whole slew of built-in libraries out of the box to get you going very quickly. Of course, .NET does take a bit longer to install than does Node.js—everything is a tradeoff—but Node.js out of the box is basically bereft of anything similar to .NET core libraries, so you have to manually build each feature you need on top of an npm package that you choose to fill the need.

You have a lot of npm packages to choose from—it's the Wild West. Unless you already double as an open source guy, you might not be used to this, coming from the neat land of Microsoft help and samples and forums. My process of finding npm packages that worked together with other npm packages—and that had working code samples I could integrate, all done very manually—was one of trial and error.

My efforts resulted in the following list of npm packages that I use both in my applications and in this book. Again, you can choose others if in your searching you find some that appeal to you on one level or another. In everything from routing to caching to authorization, you have your choice.

I broke it down this way for needed site functionality:

Basic / Core
>   Routing
>   Request and QueryString
>   Response
>   Form data
Statement management
Database access
IO / File upload
Rendering
Authentication

Thus, for addressing individual areas, I selected an individual npm package—or, in some cases, more than one used in combination, such as for generating the UI. I'll briefly summarize each of these cases in the following table and then cover them in detail later for each case as needed:

Basic/Core	Express
Routing	Express
Request and QS	Express
Response	Express
Form data	Body-parser
State management	Memory-cache
Database access	Tedious
IO / File Upload	Busboy
Rendering	EJS/Bootstrap (Bower)
Authentication	Passport

Here is a summary of the items in the preceding table:

■ **Express**   The backbone support harness for the Node.js core. It makes things like routing and sending responses very easy to do.

■ **Body-parser**   A specific tool that gives you quick and easy access to values submitted using a Form Post.

■ **Memory-cache**   A specific tool for allowing page-to-page (view-to-view) state management as a time-manageable Dictionary collection.

- **Tedious** This amounts to a driver from Node.js for Microsoft SQL Server. It was chosen for this project simply because, right now, if you are working in .NET you probably are more likely to have to connect to SQL Server from a Node.js project than to any other database. However, a similar npm package for MySQL does exist, and you can use it if getting access to a SQL Server instance is a problem for you in any way.

- **EJS** An embedded JavaScript rendering engine that will cause you to modify any HTML pages you create to instead use the file extension *.ejs* for page generation.

- **Bootstrap (and Bower)** Bootstrap is a styling engine for the UI. Bower is similar to npm itself in that it must be downloaded prior to downloading other packages—in this case, packages for assisting in UI generation as opposed to core functionality like those of npm. Bower is downloaded using npm, and then Bootstrap and any other similar UI-centric libraries would be downloaded using Bower instead of npm. The command-line commands are nearly identical to npm.

- **Passport** Passport is the package used for authentication, and it supports the typical user name and password plus Facebook, Twitter, and more.

We'll install each of these packages needed for the application in this book. Installation is simple from the command line. Open it any way that you prefer. (Just remember that if you use your Node.js command prompt from its default location, you need to change directories as I mentioned earlier.)

Make sure that your actual command-line location matches the location you entered for the root directory of your project, because npm will install packages to that location.

> **Tip** To get to that location quickly, open the site root location in your file manager, right-click the file location at the top, and do a copy as text. Then use another right-click to paste that path after a *cd* command in your command window.

From that correct place in your file system, just type the following:

```
npm install express
```

Or you can even just type the following into the command line:

```
npm i express
```

You should see something start to happen, like this:

The console should do something visually interesting in a minor way. When it's done, the console will fill with affirmations of the download, meaning you are all set with the express package.

The process is identical for every package—just change the name of the package you want to download. As you can see, it happens very quickly.

Typically, at this point you just start plugging things in piece by piece as you code them. However, as long as you have the advantage of having mapped out each package you need for your application, let's go ahead and grab the rest of the packages we'll be using as we go. So while your command window is still open, type in each of the following one at a time and let each process run:

```
npm i body-parser
npm i memory-cache
npm i tedious
npm i ejs
npm i passport
npm i -g bower
bower i bootstrap
```

You can do these in any order as long as you do the highlighted Bower install before you try to do Bootstrap. As you can see, Bower package installation is nearly identical to the installation of a package with npm.

The only line to note is the highlighted line grabbing Bower itself, where the addition of the **–g** to the command tells the npm command to look globally for resources, rather than just within its own standard library list.

> **Note** The Bower website says the following: "Bower depends on Node.js and npm. Also make sure that git is installed as some bower packages require it to be fetched and installed."
>
> If you do not happen to have GIT installed already on your system, just go to the following site:
>
> `http://git-scm.com/downloads`
>
> From there, download the appropriate version for your system as suggested.

That more or less completes your setup process for starting to build your Node.js application. It's really a perfect introduction to the world of Node.js in direct comparison with .NET. With Visual Studio, you download it, turn it on, code it, and you're off. But with open source tools, you typically do everything yourself.

You have to do extra work under this coding model, but the tradeoff is that you have all the control this way. Also, as I mentioned, with the abundance of similar packages available, you can craft your application to your specific preference even in the deepest parts of its inner functionality.

With the setup done, let's start taking a look at some code.

CHAPTER 2

JavaScript and asynchronous code

I f you go to the actual NodeJS.org home page and not just the download page, you might not need to scroll to find a code sample that looks pretty much like this:

```
var http = require('http');
http.createServer(function (req, res) {
  res.writeHead(200, {'Content-Type': 'text/plain'});
  res.end('Hello World\n');
}).listen(1234, '127.0.0.1');
console.log('Server running at http://127.0.0.1:1234/');
```

This sample is followed by a section that says the following:

```
"To run the server, put the code into a file example.js and execute it with the node program
from the command line:"
% node example.js
```

That produces output in the console that says this:

```
Server running at http://127.0.0.1:1234/
```

Feel free to try it from the correct file-location command prompt. (In this case, it will work both from where you did the original Node.js install and also where you set up your Microsoft Visual Studio path to run your Node.js project.) From there, you will probably get the output promised.

If you do, you can then launch a browser to the IP you specified. (The port you originally specify is totally up to you as long as you use four digits.) You will see your "Hello World" output on the page. Although you aren't going to be using this code, you'll do something very similar. Just these few lines of code serve to illustrate a number of things you need to know about JavaScript and also the way that Node.js expects you to use it—not to mention it also works if you really did create a server with six lines of JavaScript. This is just a smidge easier than installing Internet Information Services (IIS)! (Of course, this server isn't doing much yet, but it still isn't too bad.)

Working with JavaScript

I won't assume you have lots of JavaScript knowledge here, but I will assume you have at least some experience with it. I'll start from the beginning, but I will move quickly. If you need to do some of your own investigation to explore in a deeper way ideas and concepts I will brush across, you'll find many resources available, including whole books, websites, and discussion groups dedicated to nothing but the practice of coding JavaScript.

 Note In the same way, if you do know the subject, feel free to skim over this chapter or large sections of it. I am not preaching about a particular way to do JavaScript. I am simply showing how I do it, which seems to work to address the real-world needs I have on a daily basis as a commercial software developer.

Let's take a look at the code and see what you can learn from it, starting with line 1:

```
var http = require('http');
```

Or you can start with the first word:

```
var
```

This is a variable type declaration. Say goodbye to strong typing! Or, for that matter, say goodbye to identifying what something is by looking at it.

This is the first idea you have to wrap your head around in JavaScript. Nothing knows anything about types until run time, and even then it's dodgy. This means, for example, you can have this:

```
var iNumber = 0;
var sNumber = "20";
```

Put these together using the plus (+) sign like this:

```
var iResult = iNumber + sNumber;
```

You will get no type mismatch errors, and you will not get addition even if you hoped for it. You will get concatenation:

```
020
```

Now suppose you are used to programming in Microsoft Visual Basic.NET and you accidentally concatenate using the ampersand (&) symbol in one place, like this:

```
var iResult = iNumber + sNumber & myNewNumber;
```

Now you get this as output:

```
0
```

What's happening? In JavaScript, the ampersand is a bitwise operator that returns *true* or *false*. In this case, the output 0 means *false* and has exactly nothing to do with your variable values in code. Additionally, JavaScript is not strict with declarations and would actually let you try to run exactly the code just shown as is, not warning you that *myNewNumber* didn't exist until runtime when the code suddenly and unexpectedly failed.

> **Note** The newest browsers will now recognize the *use strict* statement. If you place this globally in your .js file, it will at least prevent the last instance just shown.

Admittedly, this is just sloppy coder coding, but it illustrates how the general idea of a non-typed language can lead to a whole mess of problems if you aren't extremely careful. I have always been a big advocate for a limited "Hungarian notation" when coding, meaning you declare an int with the name *iValue* and a string with the name *sValue* so that when you have 3,000 lines of code, you know what's what when debugging without having to dig back through your code and find the type declaration, wherever it might be.

JavaScript is a keep-it-neat idea on steroids, so it won't help you with types *at all*. If you don't tell yourself, by variable name, what this value or object is that you have running around in your code, you are making a heap of trouble for yourself.

Keep in mind that this problem soon cascades into your functions, as illustrated by this part of line 2 of the earlier code:

```
function (req, res)
```

This is a function declaration in JavaScript that takes two passed in arguments. As you can see, they have no types at all. In this case, JavaScript has to look at the rest of the call in which this function is embedded (which I will discuss in more detail shortly) and match it to an expected signature in the npm package. The npm package is just a JavaScript file library that, no doubt, contains some JavaScript object, the type of which is expected in this function as argument one or two. Thus, if you make a reference to some property of the object, such as on line 4 shown here, somewhere up the tree it fits together:

```
res.end(…);
```

This isn't exactly intuitive if you come from the land of strong typing! You simply have to know the right properties to use and how to use them. You'll get a lot of very unintuitive errors about things being "undefined" when you don't.

I didn't mean to jump around the code shown earlier, but you can see everywhere how important this idea of non-strong-typing really is within JavaScript. Danger! Danger everywhere, Will Robinson! So be advised.

Now that I've covered that, let's get back into the code shown earlier and the line where you left off:

```
var http = require('http');
```

This is the standard way of including a Node.js module in your code. Think of it as your *import* or *includes* statement. If you don't have the module installed that you try to reference in this line, your code will throw an error telling you it has no clue what you mean.

Here you didn't actually install an "http" module, so the need to do this process right here is just a quirk of this particular Node.js base library. And, as I said, you won't be using it anyway. But the *require* function call is the same in almost all cases, and it returns some object that is useful in some important way. Again, you are the one who needs to know what the object and its properties will be when it returns to you.

In this case, *http* has just one important thing that it can do, and that is create a web server using the *http.createServer();* function call. That function call contains another boatload of JavaScript information and, equally as important, information about how Node.js expects you to write it for everything to work properly. The line of code without the meat in the middle is *http.createServer(function (req, res) {});*.

Yes, this really is a function that takes a function as an argument. In JavaScript, even a function is an object. The closest comparison in .NET-land would be a delegate, which is an object wrapper around a function.

> **Note** I actually said that backwards. The fact is every object in JavaScript is declared as a function. I'll get to this, too, very shortly. I do realize that if all you have done with JavaScript up until this point is hide and show some divs with JQuery, this is fairly mind-expanding stuff. I'll keep it as simple as I can and let you run with the rest when you're ready.

Let's get back to our one line of wondercode:

```
http.createServer(function (req, res) {
  res.writeHead(200, {'Content-Type': 'text/plain'});
  res.end('Hello World\n');
}).listen(1234, '127.0.0.1');
```

The special thing about JavaScript and passing functions to functions (such as function A as an argument to function B) is that function B doesn't actually use that function per se or anything that it does. Instead, it wires that function as a *callback*.

A callback function is basically the same as a callback from your local phone company. If you call the phone company (if it's a modern phone company, that is) when customer service is busy, you will get an option to leave your number and have the company return the call or "call you back" when they are ready to service you. In other words, they'll call you when they are done doing whatever else they were doing before they could get to you. The callback function A receives the result of function B and then can act upon that result.

This concept, using callback functions in every action you take in JavaScript, is the essence of Node.js programming. It creates what is known as the *asynchronous model of code.*

Something is *synchronous* if it always runs in order, A and then B and then C. But if B is a callback function, meaning it begins to run only when function A has some final result for it to start working on, then C could run after A finishes but before B is done running, making the code asynchronous:

```
obj.myFunctionA(functionB (x) {});
obj.myFunctionC();
```

Just passing an argument that JavaScript thinks is an object like any other (!) doesn't stop code from running. So the JavaScript processor (which could be the subject of a whole book on its own if it isn't already) thinks that function A is done when whatever is in its brackets is done running. It couldn't care less about the fact that function B hasn't yet finished doing what it needs to do before function C goes ahead and leaves the starting gate.

Despite whatever complications this idea introduces to your code and data logic, it contains a tremendous amount of power and potential. At its most basic level, if function A is a web request and function C is also a web request, then C does not have to wait for the results of A (meaning B) to finish processing or rendering before beginning to run. As long as B, which is now running in its own little universe, is not touching any resources common to C, by following this model cleverly enough you can conceivably craft a way to spin a huge number of concurrently running universes, all processing their own requests in their own space. They are completely independent of any other resource and serve up webpages at the absolute optimum speed for each one.

All of this helps explain some of the anecdotal evidence I referred to at the beginning of the book, and it explains why we have Node.js in the first place. The widespread use of the callback model creates asynchronous processing of web requests, and it can have a huge positive impact on performance.

That's really all it is. After that, you do everything by hand to fit the model. Doing this, of course, would be practically impossible on a day-to-day commercial basis when compared dollar-for-dollar against almost anything with prebuilt toolkits containing everything from controls to styling to database connections and more. Hence, you see an explosion in the number of npm packages to bring those development times more in line with other approaches and, thus, the current state of Node.js development.

Once you accept all the concepts I've touched on in the last few pages, you can start to dissect what's happening:

```
http.createServer(
function (req, res)
  {
  res.writeHead(200, {'Content-Type': 'text/plain'});
  res.end('Hello World\n');
})
```

The function *createServer* is not taking any arguments other than a callback function. So somewhere in the Node.js backbone lives this HTTP object. It does what it does, expecting you to provide a function with exactly this signature, which it will then call when it is done. That callback function is expecting to pass two arguments generated by the backbone. As the names imply, these arguments will be objects you are familiar with in the world of HTTP: a request object and a response object.

> **Note** As I talked about earlier, in the land of JavaScript there is no way to know what objects are without cluing yourself in by using the name and then referring to your own code or whatever documentation you can get your hands on. These are some of the reasons this book is intended for people who have had at least some experience doing real-world web development. For a novice programmer, Node.js would be totally baffling without it.

You can see that the response object contains properties and functions you can recognize: a *writeHead* function and an *end* function that has at least one overload version that accepts some plain text to write to the response as it ends itself. In this case, we are writing *Hello World*.

One major thing to note: as written, this server will return *Hello World* for every web request it receives. That's not very practical. How to recognize routes and then do the routing is covered later. You will use the features contained in the Express npm package as the backbone for that functionality, not the Node.js core itself. But you can dig down into the HTTP object and this callback function, and you can do it here if you choose to.

Finally, you need to turn it on. That's what this line does:

```
.listen(1234, '127.0.0.1');
```

Whatever object is returned from the *createServer* function you called must have a *listen* function as one of its properties that activates the underlying server code. And that function needs an IP address and a port on which to listen for requests. The code could be written as follows for clarity:

```
var server = http.createServer(function (req, res) {
    res.writeHead(200, {'Content-Type': 'text/plain'});
    res.end('Hello World\n');});
server.listen(1234, '127.0.0.1');
```

However, the infamous JavaScript processor apparently prefers the "chained" version for reasons of its own. So use it when you can.

> **Note** Optimized JavaScript can lead to some of the most unreadable code on the planet. It is simply a tradeoff you are required to make for the sake of performance if that level of performance really does matter to you—and it might, depending on the circumstances.

How's that for one line of code? Welcome to the heart and soul of JavaScript Land—its capital city, Node.js.

The infrastructure supporting the capital city, referred to no less than four times in the one line of code just shown, is *Object-Oriented JavaScript (OOJS)*. Some objects in the preceding code are created; others are referenced by inference, and still others are referenced directly using properties or methods. Anything as important as the underlying foundation for a kingdom better be solidly designed, so without getting overly verbose on the subject let's spend a few minutes talking about some best practices for OOJS:

Object-Oriented JavaScript

As I mentioned earlier, every object in JavaScript is declared as a function:

```
function Person(){}
```

In turn, as you saw from the entire callback structure, every function also acts as an object. Some people in JavaScript Land use *Function* to refer to an object (a collection of related code) and *function* to refer to a method (code that performs a single specific action). I'll stick with the standard references, all similarities in syntax aside.

Let's begin with an object you will actually build on and use later as you go along. You're going to design a simple Sports Survey Web Application that will generate a few questions to a UI and allow users to interact and generate responses to those questions. There are a couple of what I refer to as *classes* (objects) that you will need to offer—for example, a few choices between players on a question. Those objects, to start with, include a *Player* object and a *Question* object.

A *Player* is a *Person*, so let's start with the line of code shown earlier and something common to all people and players:

```
function Person(){
this.lastName = "";
this.firstName = "";
}
```

If you are wondering when you declared that property or the fields/properties called *lastName* and *firstName*, the answer is "You just did." The magic keyword *this* has created the reference to those properties on the fly. Yes, this has innumerable potential hazards. No, this is not unique to Node.js. So let's just plow on as if we didn't have any issues at all. Life in JavaScript Land is like this every day. You get used to it by being extremely careful in your code practices.

So next you narrow down the kind of person you need, and that is a player. First and foremost, a player is a person. When you create the *Player* object, first you tell it that it is a *Person* by using the *prototype* property like this:

```
function Player () {
this.prototype = Person;
this.sport = "Football";
this.displayName = function(){
    return(this.lastName + ',' + this.firstName);
}
}
```

As you see, to make a property into a method, you just declare it as a function. Now any *Player* object you declare will also have all the properties of a *Person*, and this code will work to pop up a message box with the concatenated name of the player:

```
var oPlayer = new Player();
oPlayer.firstName = "Walter";
oPlayer.lastName = "Payton";
alert(oPlayer.displayName());
```

In this case, it seems as if you should actually call this object *FootballPlayer*. As you can see from the code, the value *Football* is hard-coded into the *sport* property, thus defining all *Players* who are instantiated using the *Player* object function call (constructor) as *FootballPlayers*. Play with this pattern as you like using prototypes to help encapsulate your code and eliminate redundancy where you can.

You can override a function in the prototype from the child class this way:

```
this.displayName = function(){
    this.lastName + ',' + this.firstName;
}
}
```

This is just like any other property. You simply set the value to something new—in this case, a new function. So you could have made the code look like this for a *BaseballPlayer* object:

```
var oPlayer = new Player();

    oPlayer.firstName = "Babe";
    oPlayer.lastName = "Ruth";
oPlayer.position = "Pitcher"; // yes he started as a pitcher!
this.displayName = function(){
this.lastName + ',' + this.firstName + ":" + this.position;
}
    alert(oPlayer.displayName());
```

It produces similar output as before, only from slightly neater code.

Again, you can add new properties and functions willy-nilly (either intentionally or by accident) to your *child class*. You are not required to implement anything at any level of the so-called *object tree* as with genuine inheritance for .NET objects and interfaces. These kinds of OOJS practices are recommended only for code consistency, maintainability, and patterning for your benefit. That means if you prefer to call your *Player* function *showAllOfMe*, feel free to go ahead. JavaScript will not care at all.

```
var oPlayer = new Player();
    oPlayer.firstName = "Walter";
    oPlayer.lastName = "Payton";
this.showAllOfMe = function(){
this.lastName + ',' + this.firstName + ":" + this.sport;
}
    alert(oPlayer.showAllOfMe());
```

However, if you're going to override every function of your prototype *base class*, there is little point in having a child/prototype set up because all it does is add convenience.

Now you have the *Player* object that will help you assemble answers to your sports survey questions. You will need a list of questions, thus the next object you need is a *Question* object:

```
function Question(oQuestion, oAllAnswers, oCorrectAnswer) {
    this.questionText = oQuestion;
    this.answersList = oAllAnswers;
    this.correctAnswer = oCorrectAnswer;
}
```

As you can see, this function is expecting a bit more to make a *Question* object than the *Player* function did to make a *Player* object. This object clearly needs some outside data to assemble properly. Again, notice the weak typing. For example, the following is obviously going to be some kind of list or array. That's obvious only because its name implies that it must be such a list to work as you logically need it to:

```
this.answers = oAllAnswers;
```

The following line is equally obviously only a single value holding, most likely, just text. (There is only one possible bit of text content for any individual question.)

```
this.questionText = oQuestion;
```

And this next line also clearly will hold a single value of whatever kind you choose that works best for you. However, just based on this, you don't know if it's a numeric or GUID-style ID that matches some AnswerID you have somewhere or if it's a text value that matches the actual content of a displayed answer.

```
this.correctAnswer = oCorrectAnswer;
```

Try to develop good habits when writing code so that you can tell what is going on in your code at all times. It will make your life much easier. I'll get back to fleshing out our "classes" later as you develop the code.

As I said earlier, my intention here is only to scratch the surface of OOJS to introduce you to its best practices for consistency and maintainability. The details of the various designs for prototyping and deriving objects of all kinds can be explored in much greater depth from a wide range of resources if you have the need and interest. For your purposes at this point, the basics of OOJS and how it is used in existing packages are enough to wrap your head around. These basics also cover how you should use OOJS to pass and manage information and behavior in your Node.js project.

You have seen the Node.js core create a server from a single, albeit slightly complex, function call. You poked around into OOJS to get a feeling for good patterns and functionality within the JavaScript world. And you combined those to analyze that single line of JavaScript code to help you better understand what that code actually does. In addition, examining that code showed you how best to use Node.js to follow the most effective patterns when building a site.

I'm sure you're more than ready to start creating something that works—an actual website generated from Node.js. You have all the background you need to do so effectively. So let's begin right now.

CHAPTER 3

Coding Node.js

Before you write any real code, inside of Microsoft Visual Studio, let's complete the setup of the project. If you take a look, you'll see that you have a couple of new folders, called *node_modules* and *bower_components*, which are the results of your command-line installs.

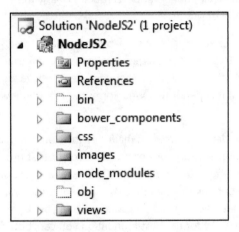

On top of that, as you'll see, you'll just be adding a couple of folders. This won't take long. My project is called *NodeJS2*; yours should look pretty much the same. If it doesn't, it soon will after you complete the next few steps.

Using the MVVM pattern

If you have any kind of Model-View-Controller (MVC) background, that will be a big plus when trying to understand how to structure your file tree. If you've worked with the MVVM (Model-View-ViewModel) version of MVC, this structure will be old hat for you. If you do not know, *MVVM* is MVC that insists you separate your View (the HTML and its spaghetti—I mean embedded—server code) from the JavaScript that supports the View. The separate .js file you create is called the *ViewModel*.

This is not to be confused with the *Model* itself of the MVC pattern, which is the data bag of properties to which the embedded fields of the View are bound. You don't have to worry about the Model in Node.js, because you don't have one. You might or might not have a data layer or business layer of code to connect to with your JavaScript.

Just to clarify, for all the fevered clamor about its superiority, MVC is just a way to generate a UI. It does not, in any way (contrary to the claims of its evangelists), force you to write your code any better than in any other *n*-tier style of application.

As I mentioned, a *Model* is just a collection of properties on which you base a *View*—hence the name. A Model should not, under any circumstances, make direct contact with a data layer. If it does, it becomes a data class and it belongs not in the UI layer of code but in the business-layer DLL. (It belongs here unless you think it should also do business logic against the data it carries and still be able to be called a "Model." That is a definition I would call "murky" at best. You are clearly mixing tiers in such a case. So much for the natural superiority of MVC!)

The point is that a well-designed, well-built, scalable application has a database, a UI of some kind, and then some number (*n*) of tiers (supporting DLLs, npm packages, JavaBeans, or whatever) containing code to which you bind your UI code. It's ridiculous to think that because you have an HTML/JavaScript/Embedded code page as a UI that it is superior to a Web Forms page, a Windows Form, or an Android phone UI.

You can build crappy Android apps that try to use data resources on main threads. You can build crappy Web Forms apps that use *SqlDataSource* and other Mort controls from Microsoft that professionals would never use that *bind* directly to data. And you can build MVC Models that fly to the moon. But by confusing code layers, you can totally debunk the idea that MVC has any structural code superiority at all. Building a solid application that follows good principles is up to you. Like anything else in life, it isn't the tool, it's how you use it. Try for the best foundation you can, both for your coding and your code structure. I won't assume you have any prior knowledge of any of the aforementioned topics and just walk through it.

Node.js follows an MVVM pattern. That means you will need an HTML file to present as a UI. That HTML file is called a *View*. So let's create a Views folder. You'll be styling the View with cascading style sheets (CSS), so create a folder called *CSS* for that. And, as with any site, you'll have images, so create a folder called *Images* for that. Now your project should be identical to the image on the previous page.

The supporting .js files you create with each View will live in the root folder. So you're finally ready to start writing real code.

Writing the code

Create a file called **app.js** and add it to the root directory. Why that specific name?

Actually, you likely already specified that's what it has to be. Check the project properties under the Web/Command Line arguments that you entered earlier during setup, and verify that's the exact name of the file you provided for startup. Whether it is or it isn't, you can call the file whatever name you want to. Just make sure the two names match: the one you give it and the one you call on startup.

In the file, build code by starting with a sanity check:

```
"use strict";
```

Using that as the first line of the file will save you some potentially buggy headaches from accidentally declaring variables (usually from typos) that don't exist.

Next, write some real code that does something:

```
var express = require('express');
```

It should be clear what you're doing here: adding the first npm package reference. The Express package takes the place of what you would have done with the core of Node.js, making life much easier for you for a lot of what you want to do.

Next, add these two lines:

```
var server = express();
server.listen(1234, function () {
    console.log("ready on 1234");
});
```

These lines should also be self-explanatory. You have a server object you got back from your *express* call, and you're turning it on by telling the server to listen for requests. Run the app, and you'll see the message and see that it's correct. Your server is running on your localhost (127.0.0.1) port 1234 (or whatever four-digit number suits you). The address *http://127.0.0.1:1234* will get you there, although you won't see anything yet. Note that you will not get a "404 page not found" error, so you're in business. You've now built a server two slightly different ways using Node.js.

Your server will run as long as node.exe is running your server file. In this case, it's running because you turned on Visual Studio. And you are popping up a console that tells you what's happening. But in the real world, you most likely would have some sort of server background service that regularly checks to see that the node is running all the time.

Note that the following would be the same code if chained, and it should produce the same working server for you:

```
express().listen(1234, function () {
    console.log("ready on 1234");
});
```

Just make sure you have the Express package referenced first. In this case, do it the first nonchained way, for reasons you will soon see.

We got this far before, albeit with different code. Now let's take it into the real world.

Our overall dev plan is to have a Sports Survey site that offers some multiple choice questions containing player names as the answers. It's always good to start with a picture of what you ultimately want. In my head, it would end up looking something like this:

- Which of these players was on a baseball team?
    1. ○ Walter Payton
    2. ○ Babe Ruth
    3. ○ Wayne Gretzky
    4. ○ Tiger Woods
- Which player used to play for the Chicago Bears?
    1. ○ Tiger Woods
    2. ○ Walter Payton
    3. ○ Babe Ruth
- Select the all time Hockey scoring leader.
    1. ○ Wayne Gretzky
    2. ○ Walter Payton
    3. ○ Bobby Orr

Obviously, it will need some styling, some images, and perhaps a login to access the page. However, my head doesn't care much about all that to start with, so this is enough to go on for now.

First you need a View to hold the HTML you plan to display and then, as always, along with that will go an associated .js file of the same name. Just add the files in the usual way using Visual Studio.

Let's call them *Survey.htm* and *Survey.js*. Put Survey.htm in the Views folder, and leave Survey.js in the root directory.

At this point, you need to tell Node.js how to find your files. Locate the following lines in your app.js file:

```
var server = express();
server.listen(1234, function () {
    console.log("ready on 1234");
});
```

After them, insert this line:

```
server.set('views', path.join(__dirname, 'views'));
```

There are two key ideas here. One idea is that Node.js has a configuration you can set at will, and the second idea is the *__dirname* value, a constant that Node.js uses to map to your local file system root directory. This is not only convenient; on another level, it's good to know that Node.js appears to have some file I/O capability. (I'll say more about this later.) For now, while you're here, do the same for your images folder, like this:

```
server.set('images', path.join(__dirname, 'images'));
```

Now you're already prepared for when you need them. (No, you can't do the same for CSS. You have to get to those files differently because they are UI files.)

At this point, you can see why you didn't chain your original server setup. You want to be able to access the object that is returned from the *express* function, and you're not done doing so.

Associated with setting the path to your Views, you have to specify for Node.js that each of them exists as you build them, one at a time. In our specific case, to inform the processor of your first created view, you need to add this line after you set the Views path:

```
server.use(require('./survey'));
```

Make sure you note the use of the relative web file path in this line rather than the standard package reference. If the resource you want to use is not in the Node.js core, the processor expects a standard relative website path. In this case, you told it to look in the root for survey, which it assumes, like everything in Node.js, is a JavaScript file. Hence, there's no need for the actual .js file suffix in the *require* reference.

Now you can turn your attention back to the newly created survey. To start with, it makes sense to be able to get the page. So let's set up a route. A *route* is a pattern by which you identify an incoming web request so that you know which page to render to the browser.

To create a route to your survey page will take a few steps. First, add these two lines to survey.js:

```
var express = require('express');
var router = express.Router();
```

First you get access to the Express package and then get an object back from a call to the *Router* method. We've decided to call this object router, and the single most important aspect of this object is the *get* function you use to direct requests to the proper View.

The *get* function looks like this:

```
router.get('/classname', function (req, res) {});
```

This is very standard stuff in Node.js with an asynchronous signature. The callback function that takes a *req* object and a *res* object as arguments is where you do your rendering or whatever else you need to do in response to an incoming URL that matches the pattern.

In our specific case, the function looks like this:

```
router.get('/survey', function (req, res) {
    res.send('this is the survey page');
});
```

For the moment, you just take advantage of the *send* method of the *response* object you got back to let you know that you got to the page. You're almost all set. The final step is to add this line to the bottom of the file:

```
module.exports = router;
```

This line tells Node.js to make the router globally available through the *exports* property of the *module* object found in the bowels of Express.

If you now use a browser to go to *http://127.0.0.1:1234/survey*, you should see "this is your survey page" output.

And that's all it takes to perform the basics of site navigation using Node.js. In this case, you sent only a simple message to render using the *send* function, but to render a complete and complex View, you use the *render* method of the same *response* object. I'll cover *render* in a moment.

Before I do, there are a couple of things to note here. First of all, this code right here

```
get('/survey' …)
```

and the pattern of the string specified within the GET is what actually tells Node.js how to route the request. Unlike in ASP.NET, the page ultimately served up has nothing at all to do with the file name in which this code lives. We chose to place this code in the survey.js file. When you call this page, you'll need all the other objects that I talked about—Players and Questions—readily available to build the page elements. So you'll place the code functions for all that in the same file.

Generally speaking, this style is my choice for so-called *code encapsulation*. All the route variations and all the JavaScript function objects that have anything to do with the survey page live in the same .js file, which is named after the intended View. And the same is true of the Home page, the About Us page, and all the rest of the pages that go into the site tree.

However, if you had chosen to place this code in the app.js file (or any other .js file that had the necessary npm package references and so on), it would run the same as it does here.

The other thing to remember is that JavaScript runs in order and so does the path-recognition tree. Just as in using .NET exceptions, you need to fall from the specific to the general and not vice versa. So you write this code as shown here:

```
var express = require('express');
var router = express.Router();
router.get('/', function (req, res) {
    res.send('matches all pages');
});
router.get('/survey', function (req, res) {
    res.send('this is the survey page');
});
module.exports = router;
```

Then use this URL from a browser as you did earlier:

```
http://127.0.0.1:1234/survey
```

The second path will never be reached and the code within it never executed. Thus, the page you intended to call will never show up.

Here's one important thing to remember: return something from every single route you create using the *response* object. If you don't use one of the following lines for every path you authorize, you'll hang your application. Your main choices of interest when sending a response are these:

- **send()**   As seen in the earlier code example, this is used to send a basic reply. Variations include the following:

    - res.send('ok');

    - res.send('really ok');

    - res.send(new Buffer('buffered simple ok'));

    - res.send({ really: 'ok' });

    - res.status(404).send('Oops, page not found.');

    - res.status(500).send({ Oops: 'something erred' });

    - sendJson()

    Although you can use the *send* method to send Json code per the fourth example just shown, this specific method will also marshal things together as Json code that are not valid Json, such as nulls and the infamous JavaScript undefined.

- **redirect()**   Navigates to the specified path.

- **end()**   Better than doing nothing.

- **render()**   We'll be covering this in detail in a few moments.

No matter how many paths you create, make sure you choose a response for each path. As you see from some of the examples, the *response* object has just about everything you need to respond to an incoming request. And the preceding list is not exhaustive; it represents only a subset of functionality. I'll cover a few more useful aspects of the *response* object later—such as *sendFile* and *cookie*—that do more than just match an answer to an inbound request.

Now you've seen Node.js work to its capacity. You created a server, and it handles real URLs. You rendered a reply, albeit a simple one. Now all the building blocks are in place for you to add more paths, more objects to handle your user state, and some styling and external connections to handle looks and data content. You need some individual wiring, and then you're off and running.

Because you're ready to dive into those individual paths, let's pause to take one last top-level view of your application and its configuration.

You already saw and employed *server.listen*, *server.use*, and *server.set* from Express in your code. The method *server.set* has a matching method *server.get*. The name server, as you might recall, is our own. It lives in a file called app.js, and that is because it is an Express Application object that is returned from the *createServer* call.

The Application object is a dictionary of name/value pairs. It contains about a dozen preconfigured meanings, such as the following ones:

- **Case-sensitive routing on/off**   Path '/Survey' is or is not the same as '/survey'

- **Strict routing on/off**   Path '/Survey/' is or is not the same as '/Survey'

- **Trust proxy**   The X-Forwarded-* headers may be trusted for determining the connection and the IP address of the client (this has many caveats).

- **views**   You set this value already for the file path to your View files.

- **view engine**   You'll be setting this as soon as you move to rendering with EJS, one of the npm packages you downloaded during project setup.

In addition to that, however, just like the ASP.NET Application object, the Express Application object can also store your own custom name/value pairs and allow you to retrieve them:

```
server.set('appName', 'NodeJSDemo');

alert(server.get('appName'));
```

Doing so gives you a global dictionary of configurable settings. Keep in mind that in JavaScript, *global* means "only as far as the page or file you're in at the time." These are not truly global application values. For that, you need the Memory-Cache package (or something similar), which I will cover later when I talk about state management.

Anyway, as for the Application object, if you need to know the enabled status of something within the collection the following line will tell you what you need to know:

```
server.disabled("trust proxy");
```

(Right now such a line in our application will output *true* if you try it.)

The number of settings within the Application object you have called server in your application are not very numerous, but they are potentially useful. Always remember that JavaScript runs in the order of the lines in the file. So, for your code to run the way you want it to, the requires statements and the configuration information typically forms the first entries in any .js file you will use as a "View Model" for your View. Then you get to the objects, routing, and rendering.

With all of those basic tools in our toolkit, let's move on to add one or two more on top and render some commercial-quality Views.

CHAPTER 4

Rendering with Node.js

Now that we've covered routing and the basic sending of a response to a web request, let's start bringing your Node.js application into the real world. In this chapter, you'll add some real webpages that allow users to interact with a data-driven UI.

Before you start

You have a couple more npm packages to hook up before you can get going. I realize this tutorial is falling into a pattern where I say, "Let's get going!" only to have you turn the page and discover there's just a wee bit more setup to do before you can actually get going. Sorry about that! Again, all I can do is remind you that this is Node.js Land where, unlike the Microsoft "add-a-page-and-then-a-control-and-click-go model," nothing comes built-in. Before you can implement anything even as simple as a single webpage for a website, you need to have a plan in mind and then set the actual tools in place. Every project you do for Node.js will be same—built from the ground up. You can come up with your list of chosen tools and try to be as efficient as you can putting them in place (such as installing everything you think you might need when you first begin, as we did). In the end, though, you will still need to assemble the parts in your application.

One of the npm packages you installed when you first set up your environment was EJS, or Embedded JavaScript. This component will serve as your rendering engine. You need to do a few things to enable your application to use EJS.

First, in your app.js file, add this line:

```
server.set('view engine', 'ejs');
```

This statement can go either above or below the line where you set the path to your views.

Now to associate the files you want to render with the EJS engine, you have to change the file extension of your HTML files from *.htm* (or *.html*) to *.ejs*.

As long as the file name of your .ejs file is the same as the name of your .js "View_Model" file (in our case, both are called *survey*) and you added the page as a static reference in the file that begins your Node.js application (which you did by adding the path with a combination of the *use* function and the *require* function in your app.js file), you are all set to start rendering the page. Again, if you already have Model-View-Controller (MVC) development experience, you can skim over a lot of this tutorial because it is similar to the MVC patterns you have seen in the past. However, as I already mentioned, I won't assume you have such experience and I'll walk you through the process step by step.

Inside your *get* function, change the *send* to a *render* and specify the intended view (in this case *survey*):

```
router.get('/survey', function (req, res) {
res.render('survey');
});
```

For the moment, just put some dummy HTML content inside of the body tag of your survey.ejs view, like this:

```
<i>Hello World</i>
```

Then browse to http://127.0.0.1:1234/survey as you did earlier. You will see your page content say hello to you, displayed in italics.

To see the effect, now change

```
res.render('survey');
```

to

```
res.render('survey2');
```

Then browse to the same page as you did earlier. Node.js will throw an error. It isn't exactly a "404 Page Not Found" error, but it's very close. In your browser window, it should say

```
Cannot get 'survey'
```

This specific error message is telling you one of two things. You might have a name mismatch in your code (meaning that nowhere in a relevant .js file is there a function called *get* that takes the exact path *'/survey'* or whatever exact pattern came in the URL request). Or the error message is telling you that your server isn't running. (Depending on your version of Microsoft Visual Studio or Node.js, you might get a "file not found" or "failure to lookup" error, but it doesn't matter. The point is that it doesn't work.)

These two files, the .ejs file and the .js file of the same name, work in concert in the same way that your code-behind page supports the ASPX file containing your HTML tags. The actual syntax of the .ejs files, however, will be reminiscent of old ASP or current MVC/Razor. Sadly, the beautiful and elegant object-oriented control you have with Web Forms that truly was a great leap forward for web programming over a dozen years ago is nowhere else to be found except in the land of .NET.

By the way, forgive an old .NET evangelist for saying this, but if you think what I just said is an overstatement, it isn't in the least. To have anywhere close to the same level of command over HTML controls in a stateless web page from code-behind that you have over a Windows Form is a mind-blowing concept still to this day. And still, in an awful lot places all over the planet, a screen flicker for a postback—that in most cases could be AJAX with the same underlying OOP platform—is a small price to pay for the speed and power of that kind of software development.

At the time .NET came into being around the turn of the century, new programming platforms were coming out every six months. In fact, if you want to know what it was like back then, we have the proof with us still to this day. Microsoft didn't even realize what it had when it released ASP.NET. Why do you think something that codes like ASP.NET—specifically, an OOP pattern (when done properly) that has nothing to do with how you build webpages in ASP—has a name so misleading it leads you to think it is similar? The answer is that, at the time, Microsoft was worried that people would be hesitant to embrace yet another new technology, so the company smudged one name into the other. Well, 15 years later, Web Forms is still here and still everywhere.

My point is only that Node.js is just another way of doing things. Some parts will be better, and some parts not so much. In some ways and in some cases, it might be superior to ASP.NET, but that fact doesn't make Web Forms anything but a rock-solid technology that has lasted for a decade. In lots of ways, for lots of businesses and clients, the extra work for building even a simple user interface that Node.js demands will not be cost effective. This whole skill set just offers you and your company new options for building solutions.

If you enjoy MVC development, this extra effort will all be no problem for you and you will be quite used to the demands and the patterns. But if you are coming from happy-go-lucky OOP Land, where you drag-and-drop from a toolbox and magically have all control properties at your fingertips to do with as you will, getting used to doing things this way will take some time. (And if you used to do ASP way back when and joyfully thought spaghetti code went away with the Y2K scare, well, the "new web" is just rife with it all over again. Node.js is as good a place as any to get back into it!)

This style of coding is known as *using a template*. Consider the two following chucks of code for a list of products:

```
var html = "<h1>"+data.title+"</h1>"
html += "<ul>"
for(var i=0; i<data.products.length; i++) {
    html += "<li><a href='products/" + data.products[i] + "'>"

    html += data.products[i] + "</a></li>"
}
html += "</ul>"
```

Versus this:

```
<h1><%= title %></h1>
<ul>
<% for(var i=0; i<products.length; i++) { %>
<li>
<a href='products/<%= products[i] %>'>
<%= products[i] %>
</a>
</li>
<% } %>
</ul>
```

These look similar, but they are different in a couple of key ways.

The first example is pure JavaScript. The line you need to add to render this list as written simply assigns the resulting HTML string to a div, a literal, or whatever control suits you. If beyond this you want to style the results, for example, you need to incorporate all of that into your JavaScript code. So it can quickly grow to be very complex, when all you really wanted to do was present a recordset to a user.

The second example is a template. The HTML tags are fixed and provide the presentation structure into which the code contained in the <% %> brackets will populate the data. As I mentioned, for anyone who has done ASP or MVC, all of this will look familiar. You will also notice that the JavaScript data object does not exist and has been replaced by this <%= %> syntax, which EJS recognizes as a property/variable value that it should fetch from the matching .js file of the same name.

This is where any similarity to code-behind ends. JavaScript knows nothing about properties, references, and so on. If you want your page to process some data when it renders, you have to explicitly supply that data when you tell the page to display. So, for the preceding example, you supply the products array during the *get* function when the request comes in:

```
res.render('products', {
        products: the ArrayYouBuild
    });
```

Then you also supply the title and any other arguments needed for EJS. Make sure they are comma delimited for each argument provided:

```
res.render('products', {
    products: the ArrayYouBuild,

title: "My Products"

    });
```

Title, for example, is used here:

```
<h1><%= title %></h1>
```

Now, assuming you had some data in the *ArrayYouBuild*, the page renders your products along with the title of the list.

Using real data

Let's begin using our real data, even if we won't render it quite this way in the final version. To start with, you'll show a simple list of players that will ultimately become one of your sets of answers for multiple-choice questions.

First, prepare the .ejs file. It will be similar to the template example shown earlier. Drop this code into your survey.ejs file:

```
<ul>
<% for(var i=0; i< players.length; i++) { %>
<li>
<a href= 'details/<%= players[i].id%>'>
<%= players[i].name%>
</a>
</li>
<% } %>
</ul>
```

As you can see, it's just a *for* loop expecting to fill an unordered list with an array of some kind. So let's provide one. In your survey.js file, create the following array:

```
var thePlayers = [
    { id: 0, name: 'Walter Payton', sport:  'Football'},
    { id: 1, name: 'Babe Ruth', sport:  'Baseball' },
    { id: 2, name: 'Wayne Gretzky', sport:  'Hockey' },
    { id: 3, name: 'Tiger Woods', sport:  'Golf' },
    { id: 4, name: 'Bobby Orr', sport:  'Hockey' }
    ];
```

This is the raw data for the array.

Change your rendering code as follows in your *get* function:

```
res.render('survey', {
    players: thePlayers
        });
```

Now if you browse to the survey page as before, you should see your list of players with the name displayed. If you mouse over the name, you should see a link in your status window with the player ID appended in the URL. It navigates to a page you have not yet constructed, so if you click the link, you will receive a "Cannot GET details" response.

So you successfully connected your .js and .ejs files to display a page containing data you built from arguments you supplied during the routing. With this major step behind you, go back and clean up what you did to make it all object-oriented as I discussed.

Convert this raw array data from JSON to OOJS format:

```
var thePlayers = [
    { id: 1, name: 'Walter Payton', sport:  'Football' },
    { id: 2, name: 'Babe Ruth', sport:  'Baseball' },
    { id: 3, name: 'Wayne Gretzky', sport:  'Hockey' },
    { id: 4, name: 'Tiger Woods', sport:  'Golf' },
    { id: 5, name: 'Bobby Orr', sport:  'Hockey' }
    ];
```

Here is that JSON in OOJS using properties of the Person and Player objects created earlier:

```
function Person(){
this.id  = 0;
this.lastName = "";
this.firstName = "";
}
function Player () {
this.prototype = Person;
this.sport = "";
this.displayName = function(){
    return (this.lastName + ',' + this.firstName);
}
}
```

The preceding code sets up your basic Person object and then prototypes your *Player* object to it. Now you declare your array and some players to put into the array:

```
var arrPlayers = [];
var oPlayer = new Player();
oPlayer.firstName = "Walter";
oPlayer.lastName = "Payton";
oPlayer.sport = "Football";
oPlayer.id = 1;
arrPlayers.push(oPlayer);
var oPlayer = new Player();
oPlayer.firstName = "Bobby";
oPlayer.lastName = "Orr";
oPlayer.sport = "Hockey";
oPlayer.id = 5;
arrPlayers.push(oPlayer);
var oPlayer = new Player();
oPlayer.firstName = "Wayne";
oPlayer.lastName = "Gretzky";
oPlayer.sport = "Hockey";
oPlayer.id = 3;
arrPlayers.push(oPlayer);
var oPlayer = new Player();
oPlayer.firstName = "Babe";
oPlayer.lastName = "Ruth";
oPlayer.sport = "Baseball";
oPlayer.id = 2;
arrPlayers.push(oPlayer);
var oPlayer = new Player();
oPlayer.firstName = "Tiger";
oPlayer.lastName = "Woods";
```

```
oPlayer.sport = "Golf";
oPlayer.id = 4;
arrPlayers.push(oPlayer);
```

Now just change your code to pull the new array, like this:

```
res.render('survey', {
    players: arrPlayers
        });
```

When you run your page again, you should see the same output as you did earlier except with the names now shown as Last, First.

You have now rendered a page using Node.js and object-oriented JavaScript. Obviously, there is more to do with the integration of the survey question structure, but you have the basic elements and concepts in place. Before we dig into them any more deeply, let's take a quick look at adding a few simple features to the page, such as images and styling.

Adding images and styling

Images are simple. Drop them in your page with a tag to the correct path for the image:

```
<img src="img1.jpg" alt="img1" />
```

Grab an image from somewhere, call it *img1*, and browse to the page. You'll see it appear.

For styling, I preloaded an npm package called *Bootstrap*, which I managed to install by using Bower. We'll dig much more into Bootstrap later, but for the moment let's just hook it up and let it work some quick magic for us.

Bootstrap is a massive collection of CSS classes that provide you with insta-styling by simply hooking the class into whatever tag you have by using the class attribute. Even something as simple as our unordered list can get a two-second facial upgrade by just referencing Bootstrap as you would a typical .css file.

In this case, you just have to find it first. Look under

```
bower_components\bootstrap\dist\css
```

and you'll see

```
bootstrap.css
```

So just add a link to it in the usual way to the *<head>* section of your .ejs page:

```
<link href="bower_components/bootstrap/dist/css/bootstrap.css" rel="stylesheet"
    type="text/css" />
```

Then just wrap your starting .ejs code in an HTML table that has a bootstrap .css table class reference, like this:

```
<table class="table">
<tr>
<td valign="top" align="center">
<ul>
<% for(var i=0; i< players.length; i++) { %>
<li>
<a href= 'details/<%= players[i].id%>'>
<%= players[i].displayName()%>
</a>
</li>
<% } %>
</ul>
</td>
</tr>
</table>
```

Now when you browse to the survey page, you'll see a much improved overall appearance. Just like that.

Granted it isn't much to start with, but then again you had to do very little so far. As I mentioned, I'll cover a few more Bootstrap features later on, but it's definitely the kind of library you want to play with to see the effects. Just as an example, drop this attribute inside your image tag:

```
<src="img1.jpg" alt="img1" class="img-rounded" />
```

You'll begin to get a feeling for what I mean about Bootstrap. Play with it, and you'll find it can snazzy-up a webpage in some very professional ways with not much effort. Reference the right .css class within the library and you're pretty much done.

So you've coded your server and constructed your first basic *get* route. You've had the correct page rendered with data, images, and styling. And you've used object-oriented JavaScript in combination with Node.js. Your basic tools are in your toolkit. Now we'll bring the application into the real world of software by connecting to external data sources, allowing for user interaction, and providing login security.

CHAPTER 5

Working with site data in Node.js

Data comes in many shapes and sizes. It can come from within your application as it works, from users, or from outside data stores. As with the rest of Node.js, there is an npm package to deal individually with each of the myriad ways data might be provided to your application.

In general, this data can be broken into three major categories, with each having a couple of primary ways that data would likely come to you:

- Data from URLs
  - Route/Path pattern
  - *QueryString*
- Data from users
  - Form posts
  - Field input
- Data from external sources
  - Databases (covered in Chapter 6, "Working with external data in Node.js")
  - File systems (covered in Chapter 7, "Working with file data in Node.js")

We'll walk through these and incorporate them into your Node.js application.

Data from URLs

The first way you'll have to deal with data in the application relates to data that comes in the URL. Even our simple example code for rendering an array that isn't connected to anything contains within it the idea that we will drill down into some detail about some item on the list. And that item is specified within the URL.

In this case, as shown, we opted to build a path that looks like this:

```
href= 'details/<%= players[i].id%>'>
```

This path yields the following result or similar as the URL path:

```
'details/5'
```

You could keep going and add as many path arguments as you like after the original. Each argument is given a name when you declare the path, like this:

```
router.get('/details/:id')
```

Or by adding to it, like this:

```
router.get('/details/:id/:name')
```

Then, in code, these arguments are accessed through the *param* collection provided by Express:

```
req.param("id")
```

Your *get* will look like this:

```
router.get('/details/:id', function (req, res) {
    res.render('details', {
        playerId: req.param("id")
    });
});
```

When you create your player and then set up the *details.js/.ejs* view, you'll have a *playerId* argument to get your hands on and display right away to make sure you have the correct data.

Always remember, as I mentioned earlier, that you must order your code to go from most specific in the path to least specific because the engine will render the first matching pattern that it finds. The warning here is this URL coming in as a web request:

```
http://127.0.0.1:1234/details/1/Payton
```

This will match the following route:

```
router.get('/details')
```

And it will match this route as well:

```
router.get('/details/:id')
```

And this route:

```
router.get('/details/:id/:name')
```

The second and third routes will never be reached if these are in the wrong order in your code file. To be properly done, these route entries need to be exactly reversed from what is shown here.

Pulling arguments from structured route paths is one way to pass and pull data from the URL. As an alternative, you could have placed the data into a *QueryString*. In the real world, this is equally as likely to be the pattern you choose to follow for building URLs internally to pass data.

You use the *QueryString* collection to access the URL's name/value pairs either by index or by name. In general, it will be just as easy to code a solution that parses its data as with the *param* collection. That being said, it is your choice, and each option works at least equally well.

To implement access to the *QueryString*, simply reference its collection instead of the *param* collection:

```
req.query.ID
```

In this case, as you see, you can actually use dot notation to access the individually named members of the collection you specified. The processing engine recognizes the question mark (*?*) as the beginning of the collection and the ampersand (*&*) as the argument separator. Thus, the route itself is still the same as the base route and the previously mentioned issues with route order in the file are not relevant.

So to process this URL:

```
http://127.0.0.1:1234/details?ID=1&Name=Payton
```

the route *get* function to render this data in all cases would simply be

```
router.get('/details', function (req, res) {
    res.render('details', {
playerId: req.query.ID,
name: req.query.Name
    });
});
```

As you can see, you simply take apart the arguments by name one at a time to get to the values contained in them. Passing an entire object this way would be done by manually taking apart the object properties to provide the necessary arguments in your assembled link to the details page:

```
href= 'details?ID=<%= players[i].id%>&Name=<%= players[i].lastName%>'>
```

Continue on like this in as much depth as required. In real-world practice, this approach is rarely needed for sending information to your own .ejs files. This is because, as you have seen, you can pass entire objects or even collections of objects in this way:

```
res.render('survey', {
    players: arrPlayers
        });
```

For connecting to external resources and assembling a *QueryString* or a route, or for taking in connections to your resources from others and thus parsing an inbound *QueryString* or route, working with data directly inside the URL is often your only option for moving that data from place to place.

Data from users

Another technique that should be familiar to you if your background is classic ASP or MVC is *form posting*. With this approach, it is assumed that there is a screen into which a user is entering one or more fields and that the entire collection of those values needs to be quickly and easily transported to a URL. To implement form posting, instead of using a *get* function inside of your .js file, you need to use a *post*:

```
router.post('/survey', function (req, res) { });
```

As you can see, *post* is almost identical in signature to *get*. Before we get more deeply into it, just touching on the subject of *post* as an alternative to *get* leads us back into taking a brief look at the four basic actions universally available over an HTTP web connection:

- **Get**   A typical web request

- **Post**   Usually used for sending a collection of data to be processed

- **Put**   Usually used for updating a single record

- **Delete**   As you might have expected, usually used for deleting a single record

A file that contains routing information will typically contain at least one of each of the four methods just defined, like this:

```
router.get('/survey', function (req, res) { });
```

```
router.post('/survey', function (req, res) { });
```

```
router.put('/survey', function (req, res) { });
```

```
router.delete('/survey', function (req, res) { });
```

As you have seen, often more than one *get* function exists within this collection. Within the *post* will be the code to get the name/value pairs from the inbound form collection. Once again, the key to this is having the proper npm package installed. In this case, it is *body-parser*. So, in your app.js file, make sure you have this line:

```
var bodyParser = require('body-parser');
```

You need the variable because you also need to place this line in the same file after the *bodyParser* declaration just shown to properly format the inbound input:

```
server.use(bodyParser.urlencoded({ extended: true }));
```

With those pieces in place, from inside your *post* function, you'll be able to access the body property of an inbound request by doing this to get your hands on the value you seek:

```
var sInput = req.body.txtInbound;
```

In this case, you are looking for a control called *txtInbound*.

To see this is action, you need to add a few things to your HTML/EJS file to activate a form post. Let's start with a button and a textbox. Just to do this demonstration, go ahead and drop a couple of input controls in a separate row below the list control you have in the page:

```
<table class="table">
<tr>
<td valign="top" align="center">
. . .
</td>
</tr>
<tr>
    <td>
<form action="/survey" method="post">
<input id="txtInbound" name="txtInbound" type="text" />
<input type="submit" />
</form>
    </td>
</tr>
</table>
```

Notice how you have wrapped your input controls in a form and then specified two important attributes—*method='post'* and *action='/survey'*—to tell the form how you want it to behave. When you submit it, you want the form to post its information to the path indicated in the action—in this case, to your survey page.

With all of this wiring in place, let's turn our attention back to the actual *post* function inside your survey.js file to have it respond to your successful form post. Again, we'll do something more useful with this later. Just to see it work, let's have it write any input value to the console:

```
router.post('/survey', function (req, res) {
 var sInput = req.body.txtInbound;
console.log(sInput);
res.send('posted');
});
```

At this point, you can pop the page open in a browser. You should see your button control and your text box. Enter any value, and click Submit. You should see the value you typed appear in the console window. Don't forget to respond with something; otherwise, your application will stop responding even if the code works as expected.

Typically, this is where you have your CRUD (Create, Update, Delete) interactions with an external source such as a database. When you return to this code in the next chapter, you'll be taking that value and inserting it into a Microsoft SQL Server database.

Now you've seen the Node.js versions of standard *get* and *post* operations.

However, aside from these basic, good old-fashioned web techniques for moving bits of data from here to there, inside your Node.js application you do have other options. One of the best of these is the cache.

To use a cache in Node.js, all you need is the proper npm package. You already installed memory-cache when you set up our application so now you just have to do the usual to enable its use:

```
var cache = require('memory-cache');
```

This component works just as you would hope that it would, similar to the .NET cache but without some of the features. To put a value into the cache, you simply do this:

```
cache.put('players', arrPlayers);
```

And to retrieve that value, this is all it takes:

```
cache.get('players');
```

This caching component also has an expiration argument, expressed in milliseconds:

```
cache.put('players', arrPlayers, 5000);
```

After the time elapses, in this case five seconds, the item will be removed from the cache if it is not renewed.

One of the most important things to notice here is that my example for storing something in the cache uses not just an object but an array of objects. The cache will hold anything you can concoct in JavaScript, and this idea opens the door to the true power of Object-Oriented JavaScript (OOJS) and sophisticated state management that's required in commercial applications. It's a pattern used in .NET to take advantage of the full power of the programming model.

The Node.js cache does for JavaScript objects what the .NET cache does for business-layer objects—it makes them universally accessible. There are two kinds of objects typically stored in the cache: lookup objects and user objects.

A *lookup object* is typically a collection of values that rarely, if ever, changes—something like US state names or US president names. A list of states stored in the database has to be fetched only one time, and then it can be held in memory after that to allow for quicker access from the application. This works quickly and easily because there is no concern that data will get out of sync—in other words, there are no worries that new data will be entered into the database and the cached version of the data will be out of date. With data that never changes, such as US states, that problem is not a problem. A routine that re-created that data once every four or eight years is also not a big issue.

Of course, this design also works for lookup data that changes more regularly. You simply have to account for those changes in memory as well as in the database—for example, by updating the collection in memory on the same button click that allows for a database update. This is one way to greatly improve the performance of your application.

In general, interaction with the database should be avoided except in cases where it simply can't be, such as for CRUD operations. Most other functions that people typically perform in the database, such as filtering and joining, can be done much more quickly by using server memory.

Picture a software application as the city of San Francisco, and imagine the only four bridges over the bay represent the database. No matter how many creative ways you navigate to one of those bridges, you'll be slammed with all the rest of the city traffic doing the same. Those are the only routes. So everyone has to use them. If you keep your database interactive operations to the bare minimum required, traffic will flow better all over your "city." That's the whole idea behind using as much cached data as you possibly can.

A *user object* holds all the information specific to a site user. That can be data from the system itself, such as profile information containing permissions, and it can be state data that is tracking current user behavior. Both kinds of information will typically be required all throughout the application, and the cache is the perfect tool to use for allowing it.

Only one difference is required in the way you manage the cache. For a lookup object, this will work:

```
cache.put('leagues', arrLeagues);
```

However, for a user-specific object, you need an identifier that ties that specific object to that and only that specific user. The standard technique for doing so is to create a *globally unique identifier* (GUID) that you associate with that user, most often on login. Then you simply prepend the GUID to your cache entry like this:

```
cache.put(GUID + 'User', myUserObj);
```

You should have that GUID for that user included in the *QueryString* on every request, like this:

```
http://127.0.0.1:1234/details?GUID=1QW3456tr4RTYUXXYiujjii45UY89898TRFReded
```

That way, you can then pull it out to get access to your user object in the cache, like this:

```
var sGUID = req.query.GUID;
var myObj = cache.get(sGUID + 'User');
```

You have a rock-solid, state management strategy in place that works for every page of your application, with code consistency, in exactly the same way.

As I mentioned, this caching technique is the only truly viable solution for all web scenarios, even in the world of .NET. If you don't believe it, try to pass a *Session* variable across a protocol change—that is, take one of your *Session* values and pass it from HTTP to HTTPS. Good luck! There's no way that coding technique will ever work. Sessions do not cross protocol boundaries. You can, and want to, create *Session* equivalents using the login GUIDs, caching, and OOP, but that's not nearly the same thing as using the *Session* object.

You can even take the idea one step further for web-farm scenarios by serializing the data in your objects to external data stores. Serialization turns the state of an object into text. So you serialize to store the data and deserialize to retrieve it. When a request comes in, you check the cache in that specific server for the GUID-related user object. If it isn't there, you pull the user state from the external store according to the GUID in the *QueryString* and reassemble it into objects right there. And then you are back to normal code operations. One technique, all scenarios, infinitely scalable.

Now you use a tech interview question to separate the wheat from the chaff—no .NET developer worth his salt will ever go near *Session*. Like form posting, it's technology from the 1990s, and .NET gave you much better ways to do the same things starting in this century, and it still does. By being well-versed in those best practices, you're fully prepared to implement the same architecture in Node.js.

At this point, you're effectively moving your data from page to page. Next let's connect to some external data and see what you can do with that.

CHAPTER 6

Working with external data in Node.js

Rendering static or dummy data is one thing, but connecting your UI to live data is something else again. If you want your application to handle the real world, you need it to track and assimilate data provided by back-end data stores, whatever they may be.

In our case, we'll start with databases—specifically, with Microsoft SQL Server. Why SQL Server? There are two reasons.

First, there is a good chance you are exploring Node.js as some sort of complement to or replacement of a .NET web application. In the vast majority of cases, the back-end database for .NET is SQL Server. Second, SQL Server has within it stored procedures (chunks of prebuilt SQL code that are held in the database that you can call by name from your code). Because these are widely used but not available in other databases such as MySQL, I want to cover the feature and show how to employ them from Node.js.

That being said, if you are trying to get things going by doing your first development with Node.js and are using SQL Express as your database, well, the fact is I couldn't get either of the primary npm packages for SQL Server, including our choice *tedious*, to work on my machine with SQL Express. Many hours of diligent effort to connect to my localhost left me with only ECONNREFUSED and ENOTFOUND errors as I played with the settings in my connection.

This is obviously frustrating at certain levels, if only because the process of connecting smoothly to a fresh install of MySQL is quite simple and happens instantly with no aggravation at all. That tells you that the problem clearly has to do with permissions. That can be a challenging area in the land of Microsoft products and is not covered in this tome. So just in case you are trying to work locally, for the moment you will also install MySQL because I know you can easily get to it on your machine.

MySQL is a *relational database system* that is almost the same as working with SQL Server but for the absence of stored procedures. As we pass through our various CRUD (Create, Update, Delete) operations, I'll include a few lines about how to work with it so as not to leave anything out. We'll also go ahead and grab the MySQL npm package so that you can work with both databases if you want to. (You already installed the SQL Server npm package when we started.) Entering the following in the correct location of your command prompt is usually all it takes to get set up for MySQL:

```
npm install mysql
```

Installing MySQL isn't directly a topic of this book but if you want to retrieve it, head over to this site:

http://dev.mysql.com/downloads/windows/

You'll find that the install process is very fast and easy. By default, you won't have any user interface in the same way that you need to use SQL Server Management Studio as a visual tool to get into your SQL Server. However, you won't need one because you'll be doing directly from code whatever you need to do.

For interacting with your chosen SQL Server, you'll need to add a couple of statements to the top of your file with some objects returned that you need in order to do that interaction:

```
var Connection = require('tedious').Connection;
var Request = require('tedious').Request;
```

Now you can get back to your *post* operation:

```
router.post('/survey', function (req, res) {
var config = {
        userName: 'fromCache',
        password: ' fromCache ',
        server: '123.45.67.89',
        options:
        {
            database: "Test"
        }
    };
 var sInput = req.body.txtInbound;
console.log(sInput);
});
```

Notice that you have now inserted your connection configuration information. To keep it simple for the moment, you can simply insert your hard-coded credentials into the code. You can already see from the example some of the potential power and ease of using the cache to hold application-wide data.

At this point, after the configuration you just try to turn it on and also provide some error handling if you don't succeed:

```
var connection = new Connection(config);
 connection.on('connect', function (err) {
        // If no error, then good to go...
        // Do some SQL here;
 } );
 connection.on('debug', function (text) {
        console.log(text);
 }
```

Assuming you have no errors (and this is where you will get them if you do), you are good to go with the database.

As you see here, the code to connect to a local version of MySQL is nearly identical assuming you have already made a similar npm reference to it:

```
var connection = mysql.createConnection(
    {
        host: 'localhost',
        user: 'fromCache',
        password: 'fromCache',
        database: 'test'
    });
    connection.connect();
```

The database *test* indicated in the code already exists in MySQL, and it has a couple of tables with a small number of fields you can use to begin development work.

Next you need code to execute some SQL. Even in a *post* insert or a *put* edit, there are times when you might want to pull back the data you just inserted, especially if default values were provided to the record during the insert. Typically, fetching data is done during a *get* operation, but we'll include both aspects here. So you need both a way to execute your insert and also a way to receive a collection and loop through it row by row.

Obviously, you can't post any data to, or pull any data from, a table that doesn't exist. So, either in your SQL Server database or in your MySQL database, create a table that will hold the player information you used before with these fields:

```
 id, firstName, lastName, sport
```

Then populate it with the following values:

```
1, Payton, Walter, Football
```

```
2, Ruth, Babe, Baseball
```

```
3, Gretzky, Wayne, Hockey
```

```
4, Woods, Tiger, Golf
```

I'll assume for the example that this table is called tblPlayers.

Let's start with the insert. I won't even talk about SQL to SQL Server without parameters. If you're still doing SQL that way, basically whatever gets hacked in your database gets hacked. You've only had a decade of warning not to use SQL without parameters and, I apologize, but I just can't generate any sympathy. The data you need to add is this:

```
 5, Orr, Bobby, Hockey
```

For your insert code, you need the SQL and the parameters along with your input fields from your form post and some *tedious* specifics such as the first line, which is self-explanatory:

```
var TYPES = require('tedious').TYPES;
 var sql = 'insert into tblPlayers (id, firstName, lastName, sport)';
sql +=  'values (@id, @first, @last, @sport)';
 var request = new Request(sql, function(err) {
    ....
  });
var sFirst = req.body.txtFirst;
var sLast = req.body.txtLast;
var sSport = req.body.txtSport;
var iID = req.body.txtID;

  request.addParameter('id', TYPES.Int, iID);
  request.addParameter('first', TYPES.VarChar, sFirst);
  request.addParameter('last', TYPES.VarChar, sLast);
  request.addParameter('sport', TYPES.VarChar, sSport);
  connection.execSql(request);
```

Then send a response that indicates something good happened. In many cases, this would be the ID just created, although for our example we are supplying the value. The whole function looks like this:

```
router.post('/survey', function (req, res) {
var config = {
        userName: 'fromCache',
        password: ' fromCache ',
        server: '123.45.67.89',
        options:
        {
            database: "Test"
        }
    };
var connection = new Connection(config);
 connection.on('connect', function (err) {
 var TYPES = require('tedious').TYPES;
 var sql = 'insert into tblPlayers (id, firstName, lastName, sport)';
sql +=  'values (@id, @first, @last, @sport)';
 var request = new Request(sql, function(err) {
    ....
  });
var sFirst = req.body.txtFirst;
var sLast = req.body.txtLast;
var sSport = req.body.txtSport;
var iID = req.body.txtID;
 request.addParameter('id', TYPES.Int, iID);
 request.addParameter('first', TYPES.VarChar, sFirst);
 request.addParameter('last', TYPES.VarChar, sLast);
 request.addParameter('sport', TYPES.VarChar, sSport);
 connection.execSql(request);
```

```
res.send(iID.toString() + ' entered ok');
  } );
 connection.on('debug', function (text) {
        console.log(text);
 }
}); // closes the post function and callback
```

With this post action receiver in place, you just need to take care of adding a couple of fields to your user interface. To keep it all clean, just go ahead and add a new view to your project quickly that you can use for your player data insert. Create playerAdmin.js and playerAdmin.ejs, and add them to your project as usual.

We'll start with playerAdmin.ejs. Add four input fields and a button wrapped in a form like this:

```
<form action="/playerAdmin" method="post">
<h3>
                       Enter new values for db</h3>
            ID: <input id="txtID" name="txtID" type="text" /><br />
            First Name: <input id="txtFirst" name="txtFirst" type="text" /><br />
            Last Name:  <input id="txtLast" name="txtLast" type="text" /><br />
            Sport: <input id="txtSport" name="txtSport" type="text" /><br />
<input type="submit" />
</form>
```

Notice the specific action we intend to implement to a route in your new playerAdmin.js file. So let's turn our attention to the route. First, make sure you add the references you need:

```
var express = require('express');
var router = express.Router();
var Connection = require('tedious').Connection;
var Request = require('tedious').Request;
```

Next, create a *post* handler that does exactly the same as the one you created earlier. Copy and paste is fine if you correct the path as shown. Also, notice that you *render* your results inside the callback of the top-level *Request* function because this is the only time you can be assured that all of your internal *Request* functions have run completely and populated the object collection you need to render your view.

```
router.post('/playerAdmin', function (req, res) {
var config = {
        userName: 'fromCache',
        password: ' fromCache ',
        server: '123.45.67.89',
        options:
        {
            database: "Test"
        }
    };
var connection = new Connection(config);
 connection.on('connect', function (err) {
var TYPES = require('tedious').TYPES;
```

```
var sql = 'insert into tblPlayers (id, firstName, lastName, sport)';
sql += 'values (@id, @first, @last, @sport)';
var request = new Request("select * from tblPlayers", function (err, rowCount)
 {
                    if (err) {
                        console.log(err);
                    } else {
                        res.redirect('/survey');
                        res.render('survey', {
                            players: cache.get("PlayerList")
                        });
                    }
});
 connection.close();
var sFirst = req.body.txtFirst;
var sLast = req.body.txtLast;
var sSport = req.body.txtSport;
var iID = req.body.txtID;
 request.addParameter('id', TYPES.Int, iID);
 request.addParameter('first', TYPES.VarChar, sFirst);
 request.addParameter('last', TYPES.VarChar, sLast);
 request.addParameter('sport', TYPES.VarChar, sSport);
 connection.execSql(request);
  } );
 connection.on('debug', function (text) {
        console.log(text);
 });
});
```

Although you could post to it right now, if you tried to browse to the page as is, you'd get the following error:

```
Cannot GET playerAdmin
```

That's because the default action of an HTTP web request is a GET and you actually haven't created a function for that. So you'll need a simple *get* as well as the *post* to render your view in the first place:

```
router.get('/playerAdmin', function (req, res) {
    res.render('playerAdmin');
});
module.exports = router;
```

It does not matter where in your file this function is placed relative to the *post* function. Don't forget to globalize the router and route with the last line.

Now you just need to add the static reference to your app.js file along with the rest, like this:

```
server.use(require('./playerAdmin'));
```

You should be all set to browse to the page. When it opens, you should see your input boxes. Enter the following values:

```
5, Orr, Bobby, Hockey
```

Click the Submit button, and you should see an indication of success. Now let's verify that's true by fetching all the rows and displaying that simple list of players using our Object-Oriented JavaScript (OOJS) connected to more SQL functions.

To select and iterate rows, you need several lines. To keep everything neat, let's create a function called *fetchPlayers* and put this code in it:

```javascript
function fetchPlayers(){
 var config = {
        userName: 'fromCache',
        password: 'fromCache',
        server: '123.45.67.89',
        options:
        {
            database: "Test"
        }
    };
    var connection = new Connection(config);
    connection.on('connect', function (err) {
        request = new Request("select * from tblPlayers", function (err, rowCount) {
            if (err) {
                console.log(err);
            } else {
                console.log(rowCount + ' rows');
            }
            connection.close();
        });
        request.on('row', function (columns) {
            columns.forEach(function (column) {
                if (column.value === null) {
                    console.log('NULL');
                } else {
                    console.log(column.value);
                }
            });
        });
        request.on('done', function (rowCount, more) {
            console.log(rowCount + ' rows returned');
        });
        connection.execSql(request);
    }
    });
```

Now you can call this function after your insert to easily confirm your data interaction was completely successful:

```
. . .
connection.execSql(request);
fetchPlayers();
```

As you see from the code, you simply wrote the results to the console for the moment, but you can clearly see where within the code you need to populate your collection of *Player* objects to display in the view. You need to take apart your resultset into individual columns and set the properties of each *Player* object to the associated values in the *forEach* loop of the *request.on* function:

```
request.on('row', function (columns)
        {
            var oPlayer = new Player();
            columns.forEach(function (column)
            {
                if (column.value === null) {
                    console.log('NULL');
                } else {
                    // console.log(column.metadata.colName);
                    switch (column.metadata.colName) {
                        case "firstName":
                            oPlayer.firstName = column.value;
                            break;
                        case "lastName":
                            oPlayer.lastName = column.value;
                            break;
                        case "sport":
                            oPlayer.sport = column.value;
                            break;
                        case "id":
                            oPlayer.id = column.value;
                            break;
                    }
                }
            }); // columns for each
            arrPlayers.push(oPlayer);
            cache.put("PlayerList", arrPlayers);
        }); // rows for each
cache.put("PlayerList", arrPlayers);
});
```

Then you just add each object to an array and stick that array in the cache. Again, for all of this to work properly, don't forget to add your *Person* and *Player* class-functions to the top of the file as well as your cache reference.

Now that you have the list of *Player* objects in cache, you can get to them easily to provide the arguments you need to render your list. Because the survey page is all set up to read those values, you used that page for your display by supplying the redirect like this as I indicated in the top-level *Request* function:

```
res.redirect('/survey');
```

Now when you do your data insert on one page, you'll get sent to another page to show the result. If you run this code and submit values to add to your list of players, you should see your ever-growing list on the survey page as you do so.

Using MySQL to do the same is similar:

```
var query = connection.query('SELECT * FROM tblPlayers');

query.on('error', function(err) {
    throw err;
});

query.on('fields', function(fields) {
    console.log(fields);
});

query.on('result', function(row) {
    // do all of the row by row work here
    // to populate the properties of the objects
    // for your array to cache
});
connection.end();
```

As you see, it also allows row-by-row access to values. Simply assign the database values column-by-column as was done with the values returned from SQL Server. Otherwise, the surrounding Node.js code is the same.

By this point, you're in pretty good shape. You've connected to a relational database management system (RDBMS) for CRUD operations, you've used your OOJS to easily manage values, and you've routed your results as desired using the cache.

But data can also be stored in the file system, so next let's look at accessing and processing files.

CHAPTER 7

Working with file data in Node.js

Data can be stored in several kinds of repositories. We've looked at databases, and we've designed receivers that could take in and parse data coming from anywhere—be it our own application or others that are posting or otherwise sending information according to specific route formats that we can take apart. Now let's look at sending, receiving, accessing, and storing files and the data contained within them.

This functionality is all supportive in nature. As a part of our website project, we have no immediate need to read and write specific files, but you can use these principles to explore options. For uploading files, I'll just assume you might want to upload images of the players to go along with the information to be displayed in their details view, but I'll leave it to you to fetch the actual images from the web as you like. Of course, you can use any files to prove the functionality to yourself.

Fortunately, a lot of this is simple to do using Node.js. To write info to a file and save it, you need to include this line to get access to the *fs* object inside of Express:

```
var fs = require('fs');
```

There's no need for another npm package. After you do that, one line of code with the *writeFile* method is all you need, along with a couple of variables passed to it containing the filename and the content you want to write into the file:

```
var sFileName = 'helloworldcool.txt'
var sMsg = 'Yo this is cool'
fs.writeFile(sFileName, sMsg, function (err) {
    if (err) return console.log(err);
// do something if successful
});
```

Now you have a new file saved where you specified, and it contains your entry.

To read info back out from the file and display it, you just use a different method of the same base *fs* object. Obviously, you typically do more than this with that data, but for the moment you'll just write the contents of the file to the console:

```
var sFileName = 'helloworldcool.txt' // same filename as last example
 fs.readFile(sFileName, function (err, fileData) {
        if (err)
            throw err;
        if (fileData)
            console.log(fileData.toString('utf8'));
});
```

These functions are simple to test—just drop the code anywhere. You might have noticed already that any code in any .js file that is not contained inside a function runs immediately when the application loads and the Node.js server starts.

I'll let you explore both the positive and negative implications of that idea. One way or the other, it's something that is good to be aware of if you weren't already.

To see what's needed to transfer a file using a typical browse button, the first thing you need to do is create the button in a view somewhere:

```
Please specify a file or a set of files:<br>
<form method='post' action='upload' enctype="multipart/form-data">
<input type='file' name='fileUpload'>
<input type='submit'>
</form>
```

To make it as easy as possible, you use basic HTML tools and then do it in a particular way. Specifically, you put your upload button inside of a form and then specify a post action and a route called *upload*:

```
<input type='file' name='fileUpload'>
```

Because this kind of functionality might be needed from several places, and putting it in a page-specific file might make it difficult to track down, on this occasion you'll add a route at the app.js level to handle all uploads:

```
server.route('/upload')
    .post(function (req, res, next) {
        req.pipe(req.busboy);
        req.busboy.on('file', function (fieldName, oFile, fileName) {
            console.log("Uploading: " + filename);
            //Path where image will be uploaded
            var fStream = fs.createWriteStream(__dirname + '/images/' + fileName);
            oFile.pipe(fStream);
            fStream.on('close', function () {
                console.log("Upload Finished of " + fileName);
                res.redirect('back');              //where to go next
            });
        });
    });
```

Yes, it is possible to route an entire application using this technique. If you think about it for a moment, you'll see why it can quickly lead to .js files for files like your app.js that are absurdly long. Separating each page and its functionality is one of the keys to keeping your code manageable—both for you and for the next person.

Notice in the preceding code sample that you are using the *busboy* npm package as well as including the *fs* feature of Express.

There are a couple of lines to focus on. First take a look at this line:

```
var fStream = fs.createWriteStream(__dirname + '/images/' + fileName);
```

Here you simply call *createWriteStream* from the *fs* object to create the necessary parameters for sending your file.

You can easily perform a test to see if this works, and if you like, you can fetch from the Web any noncopyrighted image of one of the players in the list of data you have. Then name it appropriately for the player and upload it into the images folder for later retrieval. When the player is selected, you can view his or her details.

The following lines, however, isolate for you a specific and useful feature of Node.js—namely, the *pipe* function:

```
req.pipe(req.busboy);
oFile.pipe(fStream);
```

In this case, you are using it only to send your file info. But the function has much greater value as well.

You will find that a common scenario when dealing with streaming files is that you will stream files both to and from remote resources. And often at the same time. You will thus be engaged in doing two separate but connected processes—both reading inbound data and then sending it out to a client.

No doubt, there will be times during these processes that the end client is consuming the data more slowly than you are sending it. If this likely behavior isn't accounted for, you will end up with some serious lagging performance issues. The solution requires that you include the ability to pause, monitor, and resume data transfers.

The *stream.pipe* function resolves this issue under the covers for you without you having to resort to a bunch of *myStreamingFile.on* functions to do all that synching work. The *pipe* call takes a readable stream (file) and pipes it to a writeable one (file) so that they are synchronized. It's an elegant solution to a nagging issue, and it's just that simple.

Streams can also be used to exercise more control over the file read process. For example, when you are reading from an existing file, you don't have to do this as you did earlier:

```
fs.readFile(sFileName, function (err, fileData) {
```

Instead, you can do the following, which is a useful technique in cases where the file is large and you might have remote-transfer issues:

```
var oStream = fs.createReadStream('existingFile');
var dataLength = 0;
oStream
    .on('data', function (chunk) {
        dataLength += chunk.length;
    })
    .on('end', function () {  // done
        console.log('The length was:', dataLength);
    });
```

Here you are using *createReadStream* from the *fs* object and its returned object, which you are calling *oStream*. The *oStream* you get back has some characteristics of the *on* functionality. This includes the data version, which is an event triggered when a chunk of data of whatever size streams in. This type of information gives you highly granular visibility into and control over the file-transfer process.

The preceding code should work in most cases as it is shown. The data type for the chunk that is returned by streams that are created by Node.js core modules will usually be a buffer or a string. Both buffer and string implement the *length* method.

In fact, combining the two similar stream functions, *createReadStream* and *createWriteStream*, as follows is the preferred way of doing a file copy in the land of Node.js:

```
fs.createReadStream("input/" + fileName )
    // Write File
    .pipe(fs.createWriteStream("output/" + fileName));
```

No other utility exists for doing this.

In the *end* function, you just record what the total size of the file was so that, assuming you knew the file size to start with, you can make sure you got all of it. To get the size of the file, you need to return to the *fs* object this way:

```
var stats = fs.statSync("myfile.txt")
var fileSizeInBytes = stats["size"]
```

Here you are using the *statSync* function to return an array of file metadata. One of the items in that array can be specified using the key size, which will give you the size of the array in bytes. That is the same measurement you will get from the *length* function of a buffer or string.

For processing internal text data, JavaScript contains a number of useful functions. For example, it contains *split*, which takes a character delimiter by which to divide a string and returns an array of the individual values in the string:

```
var sName = "Michael Jeffery Jordan!";
var arrName = sName.split(" ");
console.log(arrName); // produces { Michael, Jeffery, Jordan! }
```

There is also the *substring* function, which is used to get a piece of a string. You simply pass it the index start and end values:

```
var sSub = sName.substring(1, 6);
console.log(sSub); // produces "ichae"
```

Note that the character at the start index is included in the returned string but the character at the end index is not.

For more sophisticated searching, there is the *match* function, which returns a string or an array of strings that matches a Regular Expression pattern:

```
var sName = "Jeff Jeffery Jefferson";
var res1 = sName.match(/Jeff/); // produces { Jeff }
var resAll = sName.match(/Jeff/g); // produces { Jeff, Jeff, Jeff }
```

The difference in the code just shown is that the global argument */g* is specified in the second *match* line. Without this change, the function will return only the first instance of the matching RegEx pattern provided.

Unless you are intentionally meaning to be case-sensitive, such as with a password during login, typically the best way to clean strings for processing is by using the function *toUpperCase*, for which there is also a matching *toLowerCase*. Use of one of these on both sides of your equation will assure that any minor capitalization variations in otherwise identical data will be ignored, thus producing more (typically correct) matches. There is also a *trim* function that removes all leading and trailing spaces.

Each of these functions is similar to what you will find in the .NET library and will be potentially useful to you as you process information using Node.js and JavaScript.

CHAPTER 8

External authentication in Node.js

Login security is a vital aspect of most websites. In addition to having standard security access through whatever provider you choose, users now expect to be able to use a single sign-on to log in to Facebook, Gmail, and so on to integrate customized content. Fortunately, through the use of the Passport npm package, Node.js provides a solution for a vast array of authentication requirements.

To work with Passport, you just provide the request to authenticate. Passport, in return, provides standardized methods for you to then manage what happens if that authentication attempt succeeds or fails. To do this, it employs an extensible set of plug-ins known as *strategies*. Strategies can range from just verifying the username and password credentials, using delegated authentication, using OAuth (for example, via Facebook or Twitter), or using federated authentication using OpenID. I'll provide working examples of several kinds of connections, but you will see a similar pattern repeated for each.

Let's get you set up first by creating your login view and its supporting *view model*. By the way, I continue to put this in italics because I think the code file associated with the view should have a title, it just doesn't in Node.js. The term *middleware* is thrown around everywhere in Node.js and seems to mean whatever people want it to mean at the time (so beware!). One of those meanings seems to be such a file. However, the same term found in documentation for a whole slew of npm packages also refers just to a function of any kind that hooks into the package. Also, as you will see in the brief appendix to this book, on common errors that you might encounter as you go, in the land of Node.js core errors, middleware is anything that has a global reference. It isn't middleware without it. So I have intentionally avoided the term, although you will be unable to as you work in Node.js.

Anyway, moving on, the login view looks more or less like this:

```
<form action="/login" method="post">
<h3>
        Enter login and password</h3>
    Username:
<input id="txtUsername" name="txtUsername" type="text" /><br />
    Password:
<input id="txtPassword" name="txtPassword" type="text" /><br />
<input type="submit" />
</form>
```

You can see what we are expecting the application to do, which is post that submitted info to */login*. So let's take care of that:

```
var express = require('express');
var router = express.Router();
var Connection = require('tedious').Connection;
var Request = require('tedious').Request;
// routes
router.get('/login', function (req, res) {
    res.render('login');
});
router.post('/login', function (req, res) {
    var sLogin = req.body.txtLogin;
    var sPassword = req.body.txtPassword;

});
module.exports = router;
```

You've made sure you can *get* to the page in the first place by rendering the view you just created, and you provide the basics of the *post* operation. The references at the top expect you to use the database at some point, but I'll let you add that code on your own.

Then make sure you can browse to the page by adding this to the app.js file:

```
server.use(require('./login'));
```

Now you're ready to hook into Passport from your site code.

First, as usual, you need to add a reference to the proper npm package in your same app.js file:

```
var passport = require('passport');
```

Now head back into your login *post* function. Its exact signature will depend on the authentication mechanism you chose to employ. Because the typical login and password validation is the obvious place to start, the first example shown will be the *Local* strategy that accepts those arguments.

Before you begin, you need to install the *passport-local* npm package:

```
npm install passport-local
```

And inside of your login.js file, you need to add the following reference:

```
var LocalStrategy = require('passport-local').Strategy;
```

Now you have access to configuring the strategy. Authenticating requests is as simple as calling *passport.authenticate* and specifying which strategy to employ. You'll add a local route to your login that specifies that mechanism to use:

```
router.post('/login/local', passport.authenticate('local',  function (req, res) {
      passport.use(new LocalStrategy(({
        usernameField: 'username',
        passwordField: 'password'
    },
      function (sLogin, sPassword, done) {
          findByUsername(sLogin);
      })
    ));
    res.redirect('/survey');
 }));
```

There are a few things to note here. You did not go into the body for the form post values. In this case, the strategy itself can be configured to pick up those input values by field name.

Also, all strategies in Passport require a validation function that accepts credentials (in this case, a username and password) and invokes a callback with a user object. Typically, of course, this function queries a database, or perhaps some internal access control list (ACL), but in this example you'll go ahead and use a simple array of users and a *findByUsername* function to loop the array for a match.

```
var arrUsers = [
    { id: 1, username: 'walter', password: 'thirtyfour', email: 'emailaddress' }
  , { id: 2, username: 'babe', password: 'homerun', email: 'emailaddress' }
];
findByUsername(username, function(err, user) {
var user;

// match the username / password in whatever way from the array and . . .
if (err) { return done(err); }
if (!user) { return done(null, false, { message: 'Unknown user ' + username }); }
if (user.password != password) { return done(null, false, { message: 'Invalid password' }); }
 return done(null, user);
    });
```

So this unfinished function you create yourself to match your own specifications for your own system expects you to "find" a user in your set of users that matches the username you passed into it. If you find one, you then look inside of that user object for the password for a match to that as well. Note how the code illustrates the granular control you have over what is passed to the *done* function to return whatever you need to return to provide information, system access, or both to the user. Always be sure to call *done* for every login path within every login route.

Now that you have a recipe for using Local authentication, let's look at a few strategies for remote authentication such as Google and Facebook. Google has its own flavor of Passport you will want to install:

```
npm install passport-google
```

And then at the top of your login.js file, you will need to create the proper references as usual:

```
var GoogleStrategy = require('passport-google').Strategy;
```

The validation function in this case accepts an OpenID identifier and profile, and it invokes a callback with a user object. Before you can use it, you have to configure the strategy in the following way, with a URL specified for successfully logged-in Google users to come back into your app automatically:

```
passport.use(new GoogleStrategy({1234/auth/google/return',
    realm: 'http://localhost:1234/'
  },
  function(identifier, profile, done) {

    profile.identifier = identifier;
    return done(null, profile);
  }
));
```

Included in the preceding code you would create to find your own definition of a *User* is the validation callback for Google authentication, which accepts *identifier, profile,* and *done* arguments. If the login is successful, a *profile* is returned containing user profile information provided by Google. Passport marshals this information together for you into some easy-to-access properties of the profile object, including the ones listed in the following table:

provider {String}	The provider with which the user authenticated (Facebook, Twitter, or other such provider)
id {String}	A unique identifier for the user, as generated by the service provider
displayName {String}	The name of this user, suitable for display
name {Object}	familyName {String} givenName {String} middleName {String}
emails {Array} [n]	value {String} The actual email address
	type {String} The type of email address (home, work, or other)
photos {Array} [n]	value {String} The URL of the image

As you can see, the profile information can be extensive and includes child arrays of multiple items where needed. If you need to aggregate custom content, this is where you get it. The array of email addresses might give you something to match on in your own database and the rest of your site user information, thus allowing for single sign-on, which actually happens at the Google login.

Single sign-on happens there because, with all the setup done, the first step in Google authentication involves redirecting the user to *google.com*. Again, as before, to accomplish this functionality you just use *passport.authenticate* and set up the specific GoogleStrategy. After authenticating the user, Google will redirect that user back to your Node.js application using the return URL of *login/google/return*.

```
router.get('/login/google', passport.authenticate('google', { failureRedirect: '/login' }),
   function (req, res) {
        // never called
   });
router.get('/login/google/callback ',
   passport.authenticate('google', { failureRedirect: '/login' }),
   function (req, res) {
        res.redirect('/survey');
   });
```

Notice that in the first *get* function the callback is empty because it will never be called, as a result of the redirection to *Google.com*. If authentication fails when using the preceding approach, the user will be redirected back to the login page. Otherwise, the route specified will be called, here redirecting your user to the survey page.

For Facebook, most of the approach is identical. However, before you begin in your Node.js application, to use Facebook authentication, you must first create an app at Facebook Developers.

When created, your individual app is assigned an App ID and App Secret. These are your connection credentials, as you will see shortly. As with Google authentication, your Node.js application must also implement a redirect URL to which the logged-in Facebook user will be sent upon success.

Within your application, as usual, first you have to make sure you have the correct npm package:

```
npm install passport-facebook
```

Then you need to have your strategy with its essential credentials to pass into the *authenticate* method:

```
var FacebookStrategy = require('passport-facebook').Strategy;
var FACEBOOK_APP_ID = "FaCEbOOkAp1DG0eZhere";
var FACEBOOK_APP_SECRET = "F@c3B00kS3cretKe7g0ezh3re";
```

And then you need to configure that strategy properly using the preceding values this way:

```
passport.use(new FacebookStrategy({
    clientID: FACEBOOK_APP_ID,
    clientSecret: FACEBOOK_APP_SECRET,
    callbackURL: "http://localhost:1234/login/facebook/callback"
  },
  function(accessToken, refreshToken, profile, done) {

      return done(null, profile);
  }
));
```

As you see, in this case the validation function of *FacebookStrategy* accepts its credentials in the form of an *accessToken*, a *refreshToken*, and a Facebook profile. Also, it invokes the usual callback with a user object.

Here, again, you decided to return the user's Facebook profile to represent the logged-in user. In a typical application, you will want to associate the Facebook account with a user record in your database or ACL and return that user information, as well as whatever Facebook profile information you choose to incorporate into your application. The Facebook profile information, once again, is available using the same profile information properties as were available from Google upon successful login.

As with Google, the first step in Facebook authentication involves redirecting the user to *facebook.com*. After authorization, Facebook redirects the user back to this application at */login/facebook/callback*, or whatever argument you specified in the *callbackURL* property of the strategy during its configuration.

```
router.get('/login/facebook',
  passport.authenticate('facebook'),
  function(req, res){
  });
router.get('/login/facebook/callback',
  passport.authenticate('facebook', { failureRedirect: '/login' }),
  function(req, res) {
    res.redirect('/');
  });
```

Again, you see that in the first *get* function the callback is empty because it will never be called, as a result of the redirection to *facebook.com*. If authentication fails in the process just shown, the user will be redirected back to the login page. Otherwise, the route specified will be called here, once again, redirecting your user to the survey page.

For our final example, we'll look at using the OAuth 2.0 specification that has recently replaced OAuth. Dropbox, Reddit, PayPal, and many cloud-based resources that use this form of authentication each have its own specific npm package implementation. Here I'll just cover the generic version. This form of authentication emphasizes tokens. For the vast majority of sites, this means specific bearer tokens, so those will be our focus.

Again, begin with the installation of the proper npm package:

```
npm install passport-http-bearer
```

Then reference the necessary module dependencies in login:

```
var BearerStrategy = require('passport-http-bearer').Strategy;
```

Next, just as with all the rest, you have to configure the OAuth 2.0 strategy:

```
passport.use(new BearerStrategy({},
  function(token, done) {
    User.findMeByToken({ token: token }, function (err, user) {
      if (err) { return done(err); }
      if (!user) { return done(null, false); }
      return done(null, user, { scope: 'read' });
    });
  }
));
```

As you can see, the OAuth 2.0 strategy validation callback accepts the token as an argument. As usual, when you finish your internal "user matching" process (called *User.findMeByToken* in the preceding code sample), it should then call the *done* method while supplying a user. If no user is found, say so through the *done* call.

Optional info can be passed to *done* to convey the scope of the token for making your internal access-control checks. Here you pass scope: 'read' as a JSON array. This information is held by Passport in the *req.authInfo* property.

Now, to employ the strategy, just make sure you have the OAuth2 npm as well as http-bearer and then hook it into your page *get* as usual:

```
router.get('/login/oauth',
passport.authenticate('oauth2'));
router.get('/login/oauth/callback',
  passport.authenticate('oauth2', { failureRedirect: '/login' }),
  function(req, res) {
    // Successful authentication, redirect
    res.redirect('/survey');
  });
```

Using one or more of the preceding authentication strategies should enable you to address the vast majority of sign-on situations you encounter inside your Node.js application.

At this point, we've covered all the essential aspects of constructing a commercial Node.js application. So let's head for the finish line by putting all the pieces together into a working site that uses all the tools in your new toolkit.

CHAPTER 9

Putting it all together in Node.js

You now have everything you need to create your Sports Survey site. Users can log in to access the survey, which will be populated by *Question* objects and contain *Player* objects as the answers. That structure will be displayed on a view, and the answers will be tracked in memory so that you can display results.

Many of these pieces are already in place. You have your login view redirecting to the survey view if the user successfully logs in. You have code to fetch a collection of Player objects. You just need to cache and not display the collection for the moment. You will wind up displaying only a small section of it as the possible answers to choose from for each survey question you ask.

You already have your objects ready:

```
function Question(sQuestion, oAllAnswers, oCorrectAnswer) {
    this.questionText = sQuestion;
    this.answersList = oAllAnswers;
    this.correctAnswer = oCorrectAnswer;
}
function Player () {
this.protoype = Person;
this.sport = "Football";
this.displayName = function(){
    return(this.lastName + ',' + this.firstName);
}
}
```

Now let's start putting them together. From looking at the properties of the *Question* object, it appears as if the *answersList* would be an array, so let's pop some players into it and see what happens. Your first question is, "Which of these players was on a baseball team?"

Make sure that one, and exactly one, player from your list is a baseball player. You don't need to specify the player or the other questions in this case, because the question is very generic. To get this logic going, put some code in a function in your app.js that will load the list of players into cache memory when the application first starts running:

```
function fetchPlayers() {
    try {
        var arrPlayers = [];
        var config = {
            userName: 'fromCache',
            password: ' fromCache ',
            server: '123.45.67.89',
            options:
        {
            database: "Dev"
        }
        };
        var connection = new Connection(config);
        connection.on('connect', function (err) {
            var request = new Request("select * from tblPlayers", function (err, rowCount) {
                if (err) {
                    console.log(err);
                } else {
                    console.log(arrPlayers.length);
                }
                connection.close();
            });
            request.on('row', function (columns) {
                var oPlayer = new Player();
                columns.forEach(function (column) {
                    if (column.value === null) {
                        console.log('NULL');
                    } else {
                        // console.log(column.metadata.colName);
                        switch (column.metadata.colName) {
                            case "firstName":
                                oPlayer.firstName = column.value;
                                break;
                            case "lastName":
                                oPlayer.lastName = column.value;
                                break;
                            case "sport":
                                oPlayer.sport = column.value;
                                break;
                            case "id":
                                oPlayer.id = column.value;
                                break;
                        }
                    }
                }); // columns for each
                arrPlayers.push(oPlayer);
            }); // rows for each
```

```
            cache.put("PlayerList", arrPlayers);
            request.on('done', function (rowCount, more) {
            });
            connection.execSql(request);
        }); // connection on
    }
    catch (Error) {
        console.log(Error);
    }
}
```

Don't forget to add references to *tedious* to allow SQL database access. Also, don't forget to include your *Player* class at the top of the file.

Now you just need to run your fetch when the app starts:

```
server.listen(1234, function () {
    fetchPlayers();
    console.log("ready on 1234");
})
```

You are displaying the number of players to the console when the function is finished. Note how your console will log that it is ready before you get your results back from the database. That is asynchronous programming as it was intended to run—that the users do not wait to be able to do A, which in this case would be logging in, while background task B (getting data ready for the next page) is completing.

Now that you have your list in memory, you can use its members to populate the answers to your survey questions. In the case of the first question, you want one and exactly one answer to be a baseball player. Because each player has been given a sport property value, you can use that value to insert the exact items you want into your answer set:

```
var arrAnswers = [];
var arrBaseball = [];
var arrNonBaseball = [];
for (var i = 0; i < cache.get('PlayerList').length; i++) {
    var oPlayer = cache.get('PlayerList')[i];
    if (oPlayer.sport.toString().toUpperCase() == "BASEBALL") {
        if (arrBaseball.length == 0)
            arrBaseball.push(oPlayer);
    }
    else {
        if (arrNonBaseball.length < 4)
            arrNonBaseball.push(oPlayer);
    }
}
for (var i = 0; i < arrBaseball.length; i++) {
    arrAnswers.push(arrBaseball[i]);
}
for (var i = 0; i < arrNonBaseball.length; i++) {
    arrAnswers.push(arrNonBaseball[i]);
}
```

And there you have it, an array of answers to your question. You inserted exactly one correct answer among the five choices. But you don't know or care exactly which players met your criteria either way. In this way, not everyone who takes the survey will see the exact same questions in every single case. Originally, you created only five players in your data, but if your testing led you to do more than that, you will see a variety of players come up in the list as you regenerate it.

The preceding code would probably best go in your survey page. You'll see what I mean if you include it inside of your *get* function for the page and then render the page as before using:

```
res.render('survey', {

    players: arrAnswers

});
```

Granted, in this case, the correct answer for this question is always first in the list, but you can randomize this with some simple logic as you choose. Of course, there are lots of ways to manipulate your array as you like. The *arr.pop();* function will remove the last items, whereas *arr.shift(oPlayer);* will dump the top item.

You already saw how *push* adds an item to the bottom of the array. To insert a value at the top, you need

```
arr.unshift(oPlayer);
```

To search the array for a value, use *indexOf* or *lastIndexOf*, depending on whether you want to start the search from the front end of the array or the back end. Keep in mind when you do so that the comparison uses the strictest operator (===), so it produces the following "not found" example for searching the array using numbers versus strings:

```
var arr = ["1", "2", "3"];
// Search the array of keys
console.log(arr.indexOf(2)); // returns -1
```

More likely, in our specific case, you will want to use the convenient filter function found in the JavaScript array type, say, to identify all players who are in the sport "Football," like this:

```
arrPlayers = arrPlayers.filter(function(player){
  return (player.sport.toString().toUpperCase() == "FOOTBALL");
});
```

Of course, the same can be done to filter down to the correct answer (for example, by name) so that you can both insert that specific player into the array and record that same player as the *correctAnswer.* For anyone who has done LINQ filtering on object collections in .NET using delegates, the preceding code looks very familiar indeed. In fact, if you replace *filter* with *FindAll* and the word *function* with the word *delegate*, you have C#/.NET syntax exactly for filtering a *List<T>*.

You also have the *forEach* syntax, which is useful for walking through the properties of objects as you might want to for Player objects:

```
var arrKeys = Object.keys(arrPlayers);
arrKeys.forEach(function(Player) {
var arr = Object.keys(arrPlayers[Player]);
 arr.forEach(function(prop) {
 var value = arrPlayers [Player][prop];
 console.log(Player +': '+ prop +' = '+ value);
   });
});
```

The preceding code is not unique to Node.js and represents only a quick overview of arrays in JavaScript. Arrays are very useful and, when combined with object-oriented programming and caching, they form the backbone of many applications. In Node.js, they are indispensable.

You'll also notice, both here and in the production code examples, the use of *toUpperCase* for string comparisons, where it is clearly intended that you want the values to match. For example, "FoOTball" should be a match even if it has minor issues. Obviously, there are places where this practice should be avoided—such as for logins and passwords, where values are intended to really not match unless they really do match in every conceivable way. However, the approach shown tends to be the rule rather than the exception, and years of hair-pulling from chasing data that "matched but didn't match" leads me to use some discipline in these areas.

So you have your answers filtered to your question content. Let's put them all together this way using our question "constructor" function as shown next. This function expects a text question, an array of answers, and the correct answer (which in this case we supplied as the first answer in the collection):

```
var sText = "Which of these players was on a baseball team?";
var oQuestion = new Question(sText, arrAnswers, arrAnswers[0]);
```

Now you simply have to render the page using the *Question* object's data. That requires some minor changes to your *render* and also to the view itself. Let's start with this:

```
res.render('survey', {
     Question: oQuestion
  });
```

Then the page itself will need to match the parent/child structure of the *Question* object to display its data properly. Because you expect to have to track answers provided by users, you'll supply a form to submit and a post action that uses the same page:

```
<form action="/survey" method="post">
<%=Question.questionText %>
<ul>
<% for(var i=0; i< Question.answersList.length; i++) { %>
<li><a href='details/<%= Question.answersList[i].id%>/
        <%= Question.answersList[i].lastName%>'>
<%= Question.answersList[i].displayName() %>
</a></li>
<% } %>
</ul>
    <input type="submit" />
</form>
```

Now browse to your survey page and you will see the fruits of your labors. Add some Bootstrap styling, and you are well on your way to a commercial Node.js application.

At this point, you have several options for recording user input. The most obvious way to accomplish this is to pull the selected answer from a form *post* operation, which is what you set up. Identify everything properly in the view, and then use your *body-parser* to pull the user selection from the list of answers.

Assuming you put the *Question* object in the cache, by using whatever management and tracking process you decide to use in memory, with this or that combination of custom objects as you like, you have a quick and easy comparison of the user answer and the *correctAnswer* contained in the cached *Question*.

Of course, this is all just a demonstration app, and you can take it as far as you like. What matters is that you now possess all the tools needed to make any Node.js application into whatever you desire.

Sockets

There is one final feature of Node.js that can be very useful in developing web applications. It isn't directly connected to all the work you did earlier, but I wanted to make sure I covered the topic so that you truly have all Node.js capabilities at hand. That feature is *sockets*.

Sockets allow for real-time, two way communication between client and server. This feature is essential for applications such as chatrooms, gaming with multiple users, and so on. The fastest and easiest way to enable sockets in your Node.js web application is by employing the **Socket.io** npm package in the standard way after download:

```
var socketio = require('socket.io');
```

At this point, your path will diverge from using Express. Sockets require a completely different server backbone. Note that the npm packages you have connected to your Express app, such as EJS or MySQL, will *not* be connected to your Socket.io app until you connect them again manually.

To enable your socket server, add this code to your existing app.js file:

```
var server2 = http.createServer(function (req, res) {
    res.writeHead(200, { 'Content-type': 'text/html' });
    res.end(fs.readFileSync(__dirname + '/views/chat.htm'));
}).listen(1235, function () {

    console.log('Listening at: http://localhost:1235');

});
socketio.listen(server2).on('connection', function (socket) {
    socket.on('message', function (msg) {
        console.log('Message Received: ', msg);
        socket.broadcast.emit('message', msg);
    });
});
```

There are several things to notice here. You are using the *http* module to create your server instead of the Express module. Within the function that creates the server is a reference to *chat.htm*, the page you want to render when a socket message comes in. And you are also listening on port 1235 instead of on your Express port at 1234. In effect, you have created an entirely new Node.js application.

Seeing this in action is as simple as constructing your own *chat.htm* page. Capture the incoming message in the *socket.on* function into an array of messages, and the just render that array to the page using any technique you choose. You can do it via EJS as you did before or by using any of the other data-rendering engines available to you, such as Angular.js. Again, because the sockets application, in effect, is living in its own world, you have many choices for precisely how you choose to implement any aspect of the application without regard for how you did so earlier or on another port.

Conclusion

You have seen the Node.js callback asynchronous structure, how to use Node.js techniques for routing, how to render content, and how to combine all that with Object-Oriented JavaScript to optimize code management and performance. You've captured user input; pulled data from form posts, query strings, and cache; connected successfully to external databases; and accessed information using files and streams. And on top of all of it, you've learned how to add images, styling, and even authentication to a range of services.

As you can see, the world of Node.js appears at first to be a very different one for doing web development than the world of .NET. You definitely need a combination of web skills and experience in the realm of web development to master it. However, Node.js has enough common elements that, once you get past the new style, you will find that many of your standard .NET best practices still apply.

So take your tools with you with confidence, and enjoy your brave new world!

Common errors in Node.js

You'll find you hit a few typical errors once in a while in Node.js. Here is a brief list of a few common ones you might encounter and the solutions to them.

Error	Cause/Solution
ERRINUSE	Your server is already on, and you tried to start it again in Microsoft Visual Studio. To make certain you get all code changes, you will want to restart when in doubt.
Cannot find Xxx	No npm package is installed.
Cannot GET Xxx	No static entry in app.js.
App requires middleware	No global mapping of file. In other words, you need some equivalent of this in whichever code file is indicated: `module.exports = whatever;`
Xxx is undefined	If employing "use strict," this error message means you didn't declare the indicated variable. It can also mean that a variable that you expect to be in scope isn't there and you need to look at your code structure.
Cannot access Xxx property of null	An object you expect to be there isn't there. Keep in mind that you are using an asynchronous processing model and that sometimes things you think should have happened by such and such a time (such as when you try to render a page) have not actually happened yet.
GENERAL: App hangs	Didn't return a response from the route.

Index

rendering, 6
statement/management, 6
support packages, 5

O

OAuth, 63
OAuth 2.0, 68–69
Object-Oriented JavaScript (OOJS), 17–20.
See also JavaScript
   best practices, 20
   converting JSON code to, 36–37
   Node.js cache, 44
   SQL functions, connecting, 53
objects, 71
   function declarations, 14, 17
   outside data for, 19
   properties, 13
   properties, setting to forEach loop values, 54
OpenID, 63, 66
optimized JavaScript, 17
overrides, 18

P

pages
   arguments, supplying, 34
   data, supplying, 34
   images, adding, 37
   routing to, 26
   separating functionality, 59
   styling, 37–38
param collection, 40
passport.authenticate function, 65, 67
passport-http-bearer package, 68
passport-local package, 64

Passport package, 7, 63
   Google flavor, 66
   req.authInfo property, 69
   strategies, 63, 65
path arguments, 39–40
path-recognition tree, 27

paths, responses for, 28
performance
   asynchronous processing and, 15
   optimized JavaScript and, 17
pipe function, 59
postbacks, 33
post function, 42–43
   body properties, accessing, 42
   connection configuration, 48
   hard-coded credentials, 48
   of logins, 64
   receiving, 51
post handlers, 51
projects
   Express versions, 3
   npm package references, adding, 23
   server, building, 23
   setup, 31
   use strict declaration, 23
properties
   adding, 19
   declaring, 18
   as methods, 18
   of objects, 13
property/variable values, 34
protocol boundaries, crossing, 45
prototype
   base class, 18–19
   child/prototype setup, 18–19
push function, adding to arrays, 74
put function, 42

Q

QueryString collection, 39
   arguments from, 40–41
   GUIDs in, 45
question mark (?), 41

R

readFile method, 57
reading data, 58–60
redirect method, 28

About the author

David Gaynes has nearly 20 years of experience as a developer, architect, and consultant working across the full software development life cycle. He has spent more than a dozen years working with Microsoft and .NET technologies for clients of all sizes. His clients have ranged from the Chicago Public Schools and the Children's Hospital in Seattle to diverse organizations in healthcare, insurance, finance, and gambling.

Free ebooks

From technical overviews to drilldowns on special topics, get *free* ebooks from Microsoft Press at:

www.microsoftvirtualacademy.com/ebooks

Download your free ebooks in PDF, EPUB, and/or Mobi for Kindle formats.

Look for other great resources at Microsoft Virtual Academy, where you can learn new skills and help advance your career with free Microsoft training delivered by experts.

Now that you've read the book...

Tell us what you think!

Was it useful?
Did it teach you what you wanted to learn?
Was there room for improvement?

Let us know at http://aka.ms/tellpress

Your feedback goes directly to the staff at Microsoft Press,
and we read every one of your responses. Thanks in advance!